P9-DCJ-421

The Betrayal Bond

Breaking Free
of Exploitive Relationships

Patrick J. Carnes, Ph.D.

Health Communications, Inc.
Deerfield Beach, Florida
www.hci-online.com

"Tain't Nobody's Biz-ness If I Do"
Words and Music by Porter Grainger and Everett Robbins
©1922, 1949, 1960 by MCA MUSIC PUBLISHING, A Division of
UNIVERSAL STUDIOS INC.
Copyright renewed
International Copyright Secured
All Rights Reserved

Library of Congress Cataloging-in-Publication Data

Carnes, Patrick, date.
    The betrayal bond : breaking free of exploitive relationships /
Patrick J. Carnes.
        p. cm.
    Includes bibliographical references.
    ISBN 1-55874-526-2 (trade paper)
    1. Relationship addiction. 2. Betrayal—Psychological aspects.
3. Psychological abuse. 4. Exploitation—Psychological aspects.
5. Victims—Psychology. I. Title.
    RC552.R44C37   1997
    616.86—dc21   97-35071
                                                                  CIP

©1997 Patrick J. Carnes
ISBN 1-55874-526-2

Publisher: Health Communications, Inc.
                    3201 S.W. 15th Street
                    Deerfield Beach, Florida 33442-8190

*This book is dedicated to
Howard Williams and Norman Sprinthall.
I carry their voices with me.*

For information on therapists in your local area, please call 800-632-3697. For information on workshops, conferences and retreats with Dr. Carnes, please call 800-621-4062, or write The Meadows, 1655 N. Tegner St., Wickenburg, AZ 85390. For information on audio- and videotapes as well as other publications by Dr. Carnes, call 800-955-9853, or write New Freedom Publications, P.O. Box 3345, Wickenburg, AZ 85358.

Contents

Figures

Acknowledgments

There are many to thank. Pat Mellody, Pia Mellody and the entire Meadows staff, for their continuous support for my writing and research. I especially wish to thank Maureen Canning, Ray Early, Elizabeth Ewins, Peter Vincent and Lynda Grange. As primary counselors they helped hone the exercises used in this book. Without Kathy Kelley's support and office skills, this manuscript may have never become manageable. As always, Linda Holman Bentley and the staff of the Phoenix Public Library helped immensely. I relied on two experts, Nancy Hopkins and Jennifer Schneider, M.D., whose careful reading of the manuscript helped fill the gaps.

The Health Communications staff experienced a delay in the publishing process because of my transition to The Meadows. They were gracious and understanding in spite of the problems the delay caused. I appreciate the hard work of Bill Chickering, Matthew Diener and Christine Belleris in shaping and editing the manuscript. I will forever be indebted to Gary Seidler, for he has encouraged my writing, my speaking and my professional work. I am grateful for his faith in me.

I have a group of friends who watched over the birth of this book. Known as the Woman Lake Gang, they are Ann and Fred Foresman, Phyllis and Lennie Brooks, Skip and Sandy Reiter, and Leslie Myers. Their care meant a lot. My wife,

Suzanne, walked every step of the way in the making of this book. It is a lucky man who has a wise woman for a spouse.

Finally, I wish to thank the people whose stories appear in these pages. My hope is that their voices become like a chorus for a new understanding of betrayal.

How This Book Came to Be

This book started in 1974. I was in graduate school and I was in love. There was one problem, however. The woman I was in love with was compulsive sexually, acting out with other men. I was putting her through school and trying to be understanding about her behavior. I was totally crazy with the relationship. We went through cycles of agony; I'd discover her behavior, there would be forgiveness and a passionate reconciliation, then I'd make another discovery and the cycle would begin all over again.

I was working on my doctorate. I had two wonderful advisors in Howard Williams and Norman Sprinthall. The gifts they gave me in my life are uncountable, but none was more important than the day they sat me down and expressed concern about my relationship. I was just on the verge of another passionate reconciliation. Norman Sprinthall looked at me and said, "You remind me of Charlie Brown and Lucy Van Pelt with the football." He was referring to Lucy's constant effort to get Charlie Brown to kick the football, which she always jerked away at the last minute. I immediately got the point. Then he added, "There is a cure for this, you know." Pausing for emphasis, he concluded: "No more football!" As far as my personal growth was concerned, it was the most important thing said to me in graduate school.

That conversation opened the door to understanding a part of myself that took a couple of decades to appreciate fully. If it is like other periods of growth in my life, there is more learning still to come. Over time I learned that I bonded with people who were very hurtful to me and remained loyal to them despite betrayal and exploitation. This pattern of insane loyalty affected my professional and business relationships, my friendships, my finances and my intimate relationships. In my counseling work I saw my pattern of behavior repeated in others. In my research I documented how that happened for people. Gradually a map emerged for me about what the problem was and how to survive and eventually overcome it.

The problem is called betrayal bonding. Betrayal intensifies pathologically the human trait of bonding deeply in the presence of danger or fear. Writing a book about it became a challenge. First, professionals who work with trauma or post traumatic stress found very similar things to what addiction professionals found. Yet both fields were largely unaware of the other. Even worse, they used different language to describe what they knew. Within the trauma field there were those who worked with *object relations* that expanded our understanding of how traumatized persons operated out of a damaged relationship template. Yet their insights were outside of mainstream trauma research. Addiction professionals were also seeing *compulsive relationships* that had all the characteristics of addictive disorders. These relationships, however, were so enmeshed in addictions and compulsive behaviors that they would get lost in the general consequences of the addictions themselves. Professionals knew that there was often a traumatic history in all addictions but were unclear about how that affected these compulsive relationships.

Finally, family and marriage researchers offered an extremely helpful understanding of the systems operating in these relationships. The challenge was how to integrate all of that complex insight into a map most people could understand. Professionals will find a conceptual audit trail in the notes and in the bibliography at the end.

The other part of my motivation to write this book came out of a six-year research project that followed over 1,000 recovering sex addicts and their families. The results of that work were published in a book called *Don't Call It Love*. In that book I reported the stages that trauma victims went through in developing the consciousness to change their lives. As researchers we found it very laborious, tedious work, but the learning was important in that it increased the level of understanding for all those who have experienced betrayal. It is core to this book.

Sometimes I have been accused of writing books that are painful to read at some points. A number of times I have been introduced to audiences in which the person making the introduction makes the observation that my book, *The Gentle Path*, should be called "The Brutal Path." Everyone laughs, including me. We laugh out of identification because we know that to grow and change require courage, honesty and effort. I have also had people tell me *Out of the Shadows* was at first painful to read. I believe this book on the betrayal bond may also present similar challenges to some readers.

Yet I also profoundly believe that books can be transformative. At times I think we professionals only believe that insight comes through therapy, support groups and intervention. All three are important tools, perhaps even indispensable. However, people reading a book in seclusion will admit realities they are not ready to acknowledge to a group or therapist. I wished to write a book that would serve as a map for people seeking some base in reality about their destructive relationships. Such an effort requires an author to join with the reader to map out the emotional landscape. I start with the open letter to the reader that follows.

Every book I have written started with the desire to create

what I needed for myself. This book is what I wished I had in 1974.

I dedicate this book to Norman Sprinthall and Howie Williams, with thanks for all their efforts on my behalf.

Introduction: Why Read This Book?

Betrayal. A breach of trust. Fear. What you thought was true—counted on to be true—was not. It was just smoke and mirrors, outright deceit and lies. Sometimes it was hard to tell because there was just enough truth to make everything seem right. Even a little truth with just the right spin can cover the outrageous. Worse, there are the sincerity and care that obscure what you have lost. You can see the outlines of it now. It was exploitation. You were used. Everything in you wants to believe you weren't. *Please make it not so,* you pray. Yet enough has emerged. Facts. Undeniable. You sizzle with anger.

Betrayal. You can't explain it away anymore. A pattern exists. You know that now. You can no longer return to the way it was (which was never really as it seemed). That would be unbearable. But to move forward means certain pain. No escape. No in-between. Choices have to be made today, not tomorrow. The usual ways you numb yourself will not work. The reality is too great, too relentless.

Betrayal. A form of abandonment. Often the abandonment is difficult to see because the betrayer can be still close, even intimate, or may be intruding in your life. Yet your interests, your well-being is continually sacrificed.

Abandonment is at the core of addictions. Abandonment

causes deep shame. Abandonment by betrayal is worse than mindless neglect. Betrayal is purposeful and self-serving. If severe enough, it is traumatic. What moves betrayal into the realm of trauma is fear and terror. If the wound is deep enough, and the terror big enough, your bodily systems shift to an alarm state. You never feel safe. You're always on full-alert, just waiting for the hurt to begin again. In that state of readiness, you're unaware that part of you has died. You are grieving. Like everyone who has loss, you have shock and disbelief, fear, loneliness and sadness. Yet you are unaware of these feelings because your guard is up. In your readiness, you abandon yourself. Yes, another abandonment.

But that is not the worst. The worst is a mind-numbing, highly addictive attachment to the people who have hurt you. You may even try to explain and help them understand what they are doing—convert them into non-abusers. You may even blame yourself, your defects, your failed efforts. You strive to do better as your life slips away in the swirl of the intensity. These attachments cause you to distrust your own judgment, distort your own realities and place yourself at even greater risk. The great irony? You are bracing yourself against further hurt. The result? A guarantee of more pain. These attachments have a name. They are called betrayal bonds.

Exploitive relationships create betrayal bonds. These occur when a victim bonds with someone who is destructive to him or her. Thus the hostage becomes the champion of the hostage taker, the incest victim covers for the parent and the exploited employee fails to expose the wrongdoing of the boss. Sexual exploitation by professionals—such as in the Father Porter case, the Pied Piper phenomenon at Jonestown, and the kidnapping of the children from the school bus at Chowchilla—grab national attention. Yet the bonds formed in those situations have much in common with the experiences most of us have.

We typically think of bonding as something good. We use

phrases like *male bonding* and *marital bonds,* referring to something positive. Yet bonds are neutral. They can be good or bad. Consider destructive marriages as in *War of the Roses* in which the attachment results in a mutually destructive bond that cannot be broken. Partners cannot leave each other the bond is so strong, even when they clearly know the risks. Similarly, adult survivors of abusive and dysfunctional families struggle with bonds that are rooted in their own betrayal experiences. Loyalty to that which does not work, or worse, to a person who is toxic, exploitive or destructive to you, is a form of insanity.

A number of signs indicate the presence of a betrayal bond:

1. When everyone around you has strong negative reactions, yet you continue covering up, defending or explaining a relationship.
2. When there is a constant pattern of nonperformance and yet you continue to believe false promises.
3. When there are repetitive, destructive fights that nobody wins.
4. When others are horrified by something that has happened to you and you are not.
5. When you obsess over showing someone that he or she is wrong about you, your relationship or the person's treatment of you.
6. When you feel stuck because you know what the other person is doing is destructive but believe you cannot do anything about it.
7. When you feel loyal to someone even though you harbor secrets that are damaging to others.
8. When you move closer to someone you know is destructive to you with the desire of converting them to a non-abuser.
9. When someone's talents, charisma or contributions cause you to overlook destructive, exploitive or degrading acts.

10. When you cannot detach from someone even though you do not trust, like or care for the person.
11. When you find yourself missing a relationship, even to the point of nostalgia and longing, that was so awful it almost destroyed you.
12. When extraordinary demands are placed upon you to measure up as a way to cover up that you've been exploited.
13. When you keep secret someone's destructive behavior toward you because of all the good they have done or the importance of their position or career.
14. When the history of your relationship is about contracts or promises that have been broken and that you are asked to overlook.

Divorce, employee relations, litigation of any type, incest, child abuse, family and marital systems, domestic violence, hostage negotiation, kidnapping, professional exploitation and religious abuse all are areas that reference and describe the pattern of betrayal bonding. They have in common situations of incredible intensity, or importance, or both. They all involve exploitation of trust, power, or both. They all can result in a bond with a person who is dangerous and exploitive. Signs of betrayal bonding include misplaced loyalty, inability to detach and self-destructive denial.

If you are reading this book, a clear betrayal has probably happened in your life. Chances are that you have also bonded with the person or persons who have let you down. Now here is the important part: **You will never mend the wound without dealing with the betrayal bond.** Like gravity, you may defy it for a while, but ultimately it will pull you back. You cannot walk away from it. Time will not heal it. Burying yourself in compulsive and addictive behaviors will bring no relief, just more pain. Being crazy will not make it better. No amount of therapy, long-term or short-term, will help without confronting it. Your ability to have a spiritual experience will be impaired. Any form of conversion or starting over only postpones the inevitable. And there is no credit for feeling sorry for yourself. You must acknowledge, understand and come to terms with the relationship.

Professional therapists can be so focused on their client's woundedness that they will overlook the betrayal bond that may remain. Why they do this becomes easy to understand. In addition to insane loyalties, betrayal can bring forth every issue, secret and unfinished business a person has, all of which are important. Further, fear and crisis are often part of the scene. So the immediate problems come first. As a result, the betrayal bond itself may be ignored.

Finally, consider the context in which betrayal bonds are most likely to occur:

> domestic violence
>
> dysfunctional marriages
>
> exploitation in the workplace
>
> religious abuse
>
> litigation
>
> kidnapping
>
> hostage situations
>
> cults
>
> addictions (alcohol, drugs, gambling, sex, eating, high-risk behavior)
>
> incest and child abuse

These are all supercharged, complex issues. When a major sports figure batters his wife, or worse, kills her, we can get lost in the legal contest, the race issues, the fate of the children, the grief of the families and the lifestyles of the wealthy.

The fact that the victim stayed in the relationship where violence was predictable underscores an insane loyalty.

When church figures are exposed for extraordinary sexual misconduct and are conclusively convicted of financial misconduct, for believers to continue to contribute funds and participate in the church community as if nothing had happened is an insane loyalty. Or consider the fact that, on average, a woman will not contact the police until her abuser has assaulted her thirty-five times.[1] There are many reasons for that figure, including insane loyalties.

Nothing in the above list is a simple issue. They are more like a collector's ball of string—years of accumulation tightly tied to one another. An unraveling needs to occur.

This, however, is a simple book. It is designed to be straightforward and direct. Clarity is essential when the situation is complicated. You should read this book to help you clarify what you need to do. There are no magic answers in these pages, only information and guidance that will help you take action. You will find you already know much of what you need to do. You may need assurance that your judgments and intuitions can be trusted.

Unravel the tangled mess slowly, one string at a time. There is great hope for you if you do. You will acquire a depth of substance most people never achieve. This book tells the stories of people who have done it, people who have let their suffering transform them. Names and details have been changed to protect their identities. But their stories are true, much like yours perhaps. Knowing this can reassure you and confirm your judgment, intuitions and common sense. If you are having difficulty facing these issues, I highly recommend you seek therapy. If you wish to have names of trained therapists in your area, call 800-632-3697. Also, I recommend the use of a journal as you use this book. It will help you complete the exercises you'll work through in the chapters that follow.

Our world is no longer a safe place. Perhaps it never was.

Between 1985 and 1993, exposure to violence increased 176 percent for the average junior high school student. Fifty percent of the women in our culture will experience some form of sexual assault during their lifetimes.

We are all aware of the shrinking global village. Violence in other lands seems closer than ever before. Terrorism and hatred leak across our borders. No longer can we say that it's not our problem.

We know what violence does to people. Alice Miller, the famous psychotherapist, described the process in her classic book *For Your Own Good.*

German children in the 1920s and 1930s became acclimatized to physical violence. They saw it in their homes, where physical punishment was routine. By today's standards, this same form of punishment would be abusive. They saw it in the streets. Germany lost a war they felt they should have won. They felt betrayed by their leaders. Political and economic chaos surrounded them. Children learned to split off from the violence. They learned to make it unreal, which is why as adults, Miller points out, they could be in the presence of concentration camps and remain unmoved.[2]

We live in a culture with obvious parallels. A war we felt we could have won, but lost. Our nightly news is a chronicle of the day's violence, the latest abductions and the most recent infidelities of our leaders. There is a feeling of betrayal. If Miller is right, we are currently experiencing the kind of fear and acclimatization that made a Hitler possible.

Betrayal makes all of this worse. Betrayal serves as a catalyst. For centuries, cultures took pride in their tolerance. Ethnic groups lived as neighbors and friends. Then there is an isolated act of violence. People suddenly feel betrayed. Feelings escalate. More violence occurs. A vengeful spiral ends in genocide and atrocities. Irretrievable hatred and trauma follow.

Unless we learn how to handle betrayal and the torturous,

obsessional relationships that evolve out of treachery, we add to the betrayal of the planet. Trust is restored when we learn to trust ourselves and build trust with others. There is no other way. By working through whatever prompted you to pick up this book, you help yourself, and the rest of us as well.

To start, we need to understand what trauma does to people.

1

WHAT TRAUMA DOES TO PEOPLE

After a traumatic experience, the human system of self-preservation seems to go onto permanent alert, as if the danger might return at any moment.

JUDITH HERMAN, *TRAUMA AND RECOVERY*

Lois was only twenty-two. Fresh out of college with a business degree in hand, she had landed a fabulous job with a large printing firm. She was ecstatic. She worked hard. The company gave her a car. She was attractive and fun. Her hard work and enthusiasm made up for her inexperience. Plus, she had support. Her boss, the marketing director, was also young by many people's standards. Nearing thirty, she already had eight years of business experience. The company had grown dramatically and many chalked it up to her skill and untiring efforts. She took Lois under her wing and they became good colleagues and friends.

One day the marketing director left the office in tears. A memo came around saying she had resigned. Lois tried to reach her at home but there was no response to the messages she left. The president of the company asked Lois to come to his office. He talked of his sadness that the marketing director was no longer with the company. He also said that he now had a problem; he had no one to run marketing. He offered Lois the job.

Lois immediately accepted. She had mixed emotions because of the loss of her supervisor and because little was known about why she left, just the tears. Yet Lois knew this was a tremendous opportunity for her. The president told her that he had taken a chance on her previous supervisor being so young and it worked out well. Lois received a bonus and a significant raise. She threw herself into her work.

A week later the president asked Lois to his office to review her first week's efforts. Lois could tell he was not totally pleased with what she had done but was unsure what he wanted. Then he launched into a description of what made her predecessor successful. Critical were her former boss's "special" relationships with customers. In fact, for the buying agents of their key accounts she would perform oral sex. That's how the company kept business. As he talked, Lois went numb with disbelief. She came out of it when he said that their customers liked office sex in certain ways and he would show her how. Then he approached her. Lois stood up and told him that she would not do this for any price. She grabbed her personal belongings and left the company in tears.

She was devastated. Friends and family gathered around Lois. They found her a therapist. The therapist said that she had experienced an assault and would need to work it through or her life would suffer. Lois pulled herself together and responded by saying that it was only a proposition and she would simply forget about it.

The therapist was right. About a month after leaving her job, Lois started having nightmares about the company president and his office. She had difficulty motivating herself to find work. Interviews went badly. She moved back in with her parents, which added even more stress. She shut down sexually. She was critical of her boyfriend who, in fact, was very supportive. That relationship ended. She found herself continually angry with her former supervisor. She berated herself for being naïve enough to think that the company's success had anything to do with marketing. She was angry with her former employer yet obsessed with what was happening in the company. The betrayal for Lois was that nothing was as it had seemed. None of her ability, hard work, enthusiasm or creativity mattered. She had believed that people had taken her seriously. In reality management had been grooming her to be the company courtesan. How could she ever trust anyone again?

Lois was also a victim of her own ability to cope. At the time of the betrayal, she felt that it was something she could handle. Calling on ancient family traditions of facing adversity, toughing it out and forging ahead, she dismissed the significance of what had happened. Only in therapy did she start to understand that she had been victimized and admit that it was traumatic for her. Like many of us, Lois learned that she looked right at it and did not see it.

Stress becomes traumatic when danger, risk, fear or anxiety is present. For Lois, she lost in a matter of minutes all that she thought she had. Further, the insidious fear was planted that the only way she could be successful was by using her body. Her talent for business didn't matter. Plus, the unwanted advance of someone who had so much power over her well-being placed her in jeopardy. Yet Lois had defenses that helped her cope with the problem. She tended to normalize and minimize. Her body, however, knew.

When in jeopardy, our body mobilizes its defenses. All our physical systems achieve high states of readiness. Adrenaline flows. The electrochemical reactions between synapses in the brain accelerate. It's just like an automobile driven at the maximum possible speed. The sustained, flat-out performance pushes the car's mechanical system past its limits. Pretty soon, things start to break down. Our bodies and minds will react the same way. When pushed past their limits, they begin to fall apart. Unlike a car, however, our bodies and minds can regenerate and recover. Some traumas that occur as a result of betrayal create damage that is residual. That is, we do not see it or understand it until later. Some traumas, especially over time, can alter how our systems operate.

Two factors are essential in understanding traumatic experiences: how far our systems are stretched and for how long. Figure 1.1 helps us understand how these two factors interact. Some events happen only once or just a few times, but the impact is so great that trauma occurs. The experience Lois had with the president of the company only lasted a few minutes, but the impact was significant and enduring. Rape, accident, assault and some types of child molestation fit this extreme form of trauma. So would being terminated without warning from a job after years of loyal service and excellent performance.

Figure 1.1. Impact of Abuse

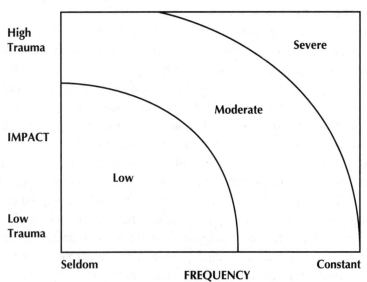

Some trauma experiences are relatively minor, but they happen every day. The hurt accumulates. Many acts of child neglect, for example, in themselves are not that serious. Every parent has moments of not being able to cover all the bases. A consistent pattern of neglect, however, creates incredible anxiety in a child and leaves serious lifelong wounds. Other examples include living in a toxic marriage or working in a toxic corporation. Little acts of degradation, manipulation, secrecy and shame on a daily basis take their toll. Trauma by accumulation sneaks up on its victims.

The compromises we make to trauma can deaden us over time. As one man described his recovery from a traumatizing marriage: "It was a full year after we split when I realized that my back felt different. It was relaxed and I could bend without effort. I had spent so many years braced for the next outburst, my back muscles were always tensed up. I never realized that while I was married." It's like walking into a room with a bad smell. The longer you stay in the room, the more the smell will seem to dissipate. Your olfactory system actually adjusts to the offensive odor. It's only by leaving the room that you will recover your sensitivity to the odor. It's the same with high stress, danger or anxiety; your body and mind will adjust— and pay for it. Only after being away from traumatic circumstances will your sensitivity return.

Betrayals that cause horrendous and long-lasting traumas are the worst. Such was the Holocaust, or Vietnam, or Russia after Stalin's purge followed by the Nazi invasion. These emotional scars can be so severe that generations descended from those surviving will react in ways that still reflect the original trauma. No amount of what appears to be normal makes it safe. Patterns and attitudes evolve far beyond the individual and are incorporated into the fabric of family and society.

How does trauma continue to act on us if things return to normal? There are eight predominant ways that trauma continues to affect people over time. They are:

trauma reaction
trauma arousal
trauma blocking
trauma splitting
trauma abstinence
trauma shame
trauma repetition
trauma bonds

While this book will focus on the insane loyalties of betrayal bonding, it is important to understand the other seven dysfunctional options that people have to cope with betrayal. These options often become significant allies of one another. So if you have one, you probably have some of the others as well. In the interests of understanding how these work together we need to understand each separately.

TRAUMA REACTION

A man finds himself being shaken awake by his wife. He is standing in the hallway outside of their bedroom. He has his old army battle fatigues on, left over from his days in Vietnam. He was hearing battle sounds—the chattering of M50s, the dull thuds of mortar fire, ear-splitting artillery. He is experiencing all the fear, the sweat and mind-numbing exhaustion of battle. When his wife wakes him he is not sure where he is. The battle seemed so real. Yet here he is twenty-three years later at 2 A.M. standing in his home. He has no idea what he was doing in the hallway or how or even why he had put on his fatigues. Scared, stunned and doubting his reality, he is helped by his wife back to bed. It takes days for him to settle down. He wonders if he is losing his sanity. He drinks heavily to calm himself.

War is a sustained, horrifying experience. In earlier wars we used the term *battle fatigue*. What that meant was that the coping mechanisms of soldiers became overwhelmed to the extent that they could not function. Now remember that the brain, body and nervous system will adjust. They will acclimatize. So for survival the soldier will continually bury the horrifying experiences into compartments in the brain. Later— sometimes many years—the compartments start to leak. The veteran reexperiences the terror, at times with the same realism of the original experience. Therapists call this Post-Traumatic Stress Disorder, or PTSD. The stress of the trauma continues long after the actual traumatic event.

PTSD can occur after any overwhelming and fear-filled event. Survivors of childhood sexual abuse will have nightmares about being sexually assaulted at the same time of night that the original assault took place. Or they will see someone, or something will happen that reminds them of those super-charged events, and it will trigger a flashback—a very real daydream—with all the original feelings. After the flashback it is very difficult for them to function as if nothing has happened. People around the survivor become very confused because something obviously has happened, but they have no idea what.

A much more minor variant of this theme occurs when people dream of taking a test in school for which they are not prepared. This common experience many have had reflects the stress of school exams. These dreams can be triggered by current stress experiences that require preparation. Similarly, the sexual abuse survivor may have difficulty being sexual as an adult because of the feelings that come back about those early terrifying experiences. Or consider how startled veterans can be when you touch them and they did not know you were there. The trigger is surprise contact—of which one type is ambush.

The deeper and more problematic issue with PTSD is how the alarm system of the brain is activated. Fear causes extraordinary changes in your neurological system and your organs—

especially the brain. In abused children we know that the actual biological tissues of the brain are altered. Recent research on Vietnam vets also revealed changes in the brain. Sustained or overwhelming fear activates and mobilizes our entire system.

Researchers in human attachment and bonding have long known that neglect and rejection of a child will create anxiety. The child fearfully asks, "what will happen to me?" Even early studies of monkeys who were neglected showed that they became extremely reactive, violent, antisocial and even compulsive sexually. Therein is the problem. Most people can have an emergency, respond well, and return to normal. But when the trauma is overwhelming and/or sustained, the body's ability to stay in an alarm state is enhanced. The alarm state starts to feel "normal." A metaphor would be an accelerator on a car that sticks. You may accelerate, but slowing down again becomes a problem. And some trauma victims live with their throttles stuck wide open. The result is highly reactive, difficult people who do not want to be the way they are. Their lives are characterized by overreaction (angry outbursts, distrust of others, excessive behavior) and disturbed relationships (short-term relationships, idealizing others until the alarms kick in and then they hate the same people they once thought were so great). Therapists will talk of *borderline personalities.* Borderline personalities are people who have been hurt so badly they are afraid and on maximum alert—all the time.

Here are some characteristics of PTSD reactivity:

> recurrent and unwanted (intrusive) recollections of experiences
>
> periods of sleeplessness
>
> sudden "real" memories (vivid, distracting)
>
> extremely cautious of surroundings

startled more easily than others

distressing dreams about experiences

flashback episodes—acting or feeling as if the experience is happening in the present

distress when exposed to reminders of experiences like anniversaries, places or symbols

outbursts of anger and irritability

distrustful of others

physical reactions to reminders of experiences (breaking out in cold sweat, trouble breathing, etc.)

Living so reactively takes a toll on the body. For example, women who were sexually abused as children are eight times more likely to have cancer than women who were not abused. Some researchers make a strong case that the impact of trauma is encoded right down to the cellular level.

In the case of Lois, who was a secure, healthy adult, betrayal generated such fear and distrust that it took years to overcome the impact. If there is enough time and sufficient fear, the impact can be highly addictive.

TRAUMA AROUSAL

Some soldiers in Vietnam used sex as a way to escape the horror of war. They experienced sex in ways that were not reproducible in a peace-time country. High-risk sex became like a drug. It stimulated the system (like amphetamines) and dulled the pain. Coming home meant they could find no parallel experience. So they simply became violent. It was the closest way they could reexperience that rush.

Some girls had their first sexual experiences under scary or even violent conditions. They found it pleasurable and felt responsible for what happened. As adults, the only way they could be orgasmic was when a man was hurting them. Their behavior became supercharged and highly addictive. They may work as prostitutes or hit the S and M clubs. Either way they find willing partners who will revictimize them.

Some executives, in an effort to compensate for horrible experiences as children, find an exhilaration in the climb to power. As CEOs of billion-dollar corporations, they only feel alive when dealing with crisis or huge risk. Leveraged buyouts, takeovers and acquisitions become the "bets" of just another form of compulsive gambling. Hooked on the stress of extraordinary power and the risk of losing everything, they cannot leave their jobs. Deal making twenty hours a day, they can hardly sleep or be with their families. They play with traumatic possibility and cannot leave it alone. For recreation they love high-speed motorcycles, sky-diving and other high-risk diversions.

Some professionals (clergy, physicians, attorneys) will have sex with those entrusted to their care (parishioners, patients, clients). Some in these professions develop a pattern of high-risk sex that is clearly addictive. Most were sexually abused as children and learned to connect their sexuality with fear. So as adults, they feel most sexual when it is dangerous or risky. One of the characteristics is that with each episode they take a greater risk—until they are inevitably caught.

Addiction specialists talk about the arousal neuropathway of addiction. Gambling, high-risk sex, stimulant drugs and high-risk activities serve as examples of this category. Stimulation and pleasure compensate for pain and emptiness. In sex alone the possibilities are endless: sex offending, sadomasochism, prostitution and anonymous sex—all rely on danger and/or fear to escalate the sexual high. Some relationships are saturated with arousal escalators—supercharged sex, violence, dramatic exits, passionate reconciliations, secrets and threats of abandonment—all in the context of "if anybody ever found out about this there would be hell to pay." This is why soap operas can be so compelling. They provide vicarious arousal with scripts based on betrayal. As we shall see, high arousal that comes from fear and danger can be an important ally of betrayal bonding.

Trauma pleasure is seeking or finding pleasure and stimulation in the presence of extreme danger, violence, risk or shame. It is a frequent outcome of betrayal and trauma. Signs of its presence are:

> engaging in high-risk, thrill-seeking behaviors such as skydiving or race-car driving
>
> seeking more risk because the last jolt of excitement was not enough
>
> difficulty being alone, calm or in low-stress environments
>
> using drugs like cocaine or amphetamines to speed things up or to heighten high-risk activities
>
> feeling sexual when frightened or when violence occurs
>
> seeking high-risk sex
>
> loving to gamble on outcomes
>
> difficulty completing sustained, steady tasks
>
> seeking danger
>
> constant searching for all-or-nothing situations
>
> associating with people who are dangerous to you

Arousal accesses a neuropathway that is very compelling. If your brain adjusts to it, you would need the stimulation simply to feel normal. Then it can become addictive and interfere with your life. You will not want to give it up. The alarm state induced by trauma becomes the gateway to many forms of addictive arousal. Yet there are other strategies for coping with trauma that also can become addictive, including efforts to block the trauma out.

TRAUMA BLOCKING

Numbing. Comforting. Relaxing. Anesthetizing. Anything to escape the uncomfortable feelings. High arousal? Something to calm the nerves. Slow down. Bad memories? Anything to obliterate the interior world. An analgesic fix to make it bearable. Some use alcohol. Some use drugs. Some do both. Compulsive eating creates comfort and drowsiness. Watching mind-numbing TV wastes time but avoids reality. Excessive sleeping becomes like a butterfly in a cocoon, only there is no intention of coming out.

Cheryl was a domestic abuse victim. She was in court eleven times because her husband had assaulted her. She felt terrible shame. Every time he beat her he screamed about it being her fault because she was so heavy. She felt the accusations were true. She knew she had problems with food and that she needed to do something. But it helped her get through the day. Besides, it was the one thing he could not control. There was an added dividend: Being fat made her sexually unattractive. She hated sex. She was an incest victim. Food was protection. Food was comfort.

Now there was the new crisis. One of the kids had told a counselor at school that her father (Cheryl's husband) was being sexual with her at night. The family had been reported to child protection. Now they were in treatment as a family. Cheryl had to go to a group of new incest moms. The therapist asked about food issues. Nine out of the eleven moms had undergone intestinal bypass surgery. Cheryl got the message. Eating was more than a self-control issue. She made it into a way to keep safe and block pain. As she progressed in treatment, she started to eat differently, and memories of her own childhood experience became more clear as well as memories she had forgotten.

Survivors block their pain. One of the leading factors in relapse for alcoholics is that as they get sober, their memories return. Rather than face the pain, they start drinking again. More and more studies show that alcoholics may switch to other addictions. Addiction becomes a solution to the trauma. The neuropathway involved here relates to a phenomenon called *satiation*. Behaviors and substances that induce calming, relaxing and numbing create electrochemical reactions in the brain that serve as analgesic "fixes." The neurochemical bottom line is anxiety reduction. For the trauma survivor this means avoiding the fear and numbing the pain. Addiction therapists use the term *compulsive* to describe the repetitive efforts to calm the mind. The problem here is that again the brain will adjust and the compulsive behavior will become necessary in order to feel normal. Then it is hard to stop because it has transformed to addiction.

Trauma blocking is an effort to numb, block out or reduce residual feelings due to trauma. Signs of satiation or efforts to block include:

excessive drinking

use of depressant drugs or "downers"

using TV, reading or hobbies as a way to numb out

compulsive eating

excessive sleeping

compulsive working, especially at unrewarding jobs

compulsive exercise

bingeing (with any of the above) when things are difficult

Any trauma of sufficient magnitude will create this response in your neuropathways. In alcoholism, for example, much research indicates that alcoholics (and indeed, addicts of all kinds) probably are born with an insufficiency of certain receptor sites in the brain. That's why alcoholics can often list other alcoholics in their families, going back many generations. Being raised in an alcoholic home is also traumatic. All these factors are commonly recognized. In Vietnam, however, we had young kids with no history of alcohol or drug abuse in the family and a stable history of emotional health who came back from the war drug addicts and alcoholics. Their ability to function became impaired. Simply said, the war overwhelmed them. They used drugs and alcohol to cope, and their brains accommodated.

Survivors often use a combination of strategies to cope. A common pattern is to use high-arousal activities of intensity, pleasure or stress and then follow with blocking strategies to balance the arousal. Drug addicts, for example, will mix uppers and downers. Or consider the man who is having anonymous, high-risk sex with other men in parks and streets. When he returns home ashamed and exhausted but cannot sleep because of the excitement, he has learned to drink a six-pack and eat until his stomach is uncomfortably distended. He passes out, oblivious. Caught up in vicious cycles of arousal and blocking, his behaviors serve as a one-two punch to the painful memories of his childhood sexual abuse. He is caught. His memories will never relent. And his addictions will kill him—one way or another.

TRAUMA SPLITTING

Escape. Individuals can find another reality to go to if the one they are in is too painful. This is like the Enterprise holodeck on *Star Trek*. When members of the crew are distraught or need a break, they go to the holodeck and create a holographic fantasy that seems very real. Many episodes use the holodeck as a counterpoint or even a plot. At the end of each adventure, however, the routine of being on a Federation starship returns, as do the problems.

There are countless similar stories told by children who were sexually assaulted. They recount how they would imagine themselves flying around the room or doing something they liked as they were being fondled or penetrated. They were separating themselves from a reality too painful to bear. At the time it was an important coping strategy. Therapists call this *splitting*—victims learn to split off the uncomfortable reality or dissociate from the experience. They do this by focusing on another reality or by creating an unreality or fantasy. When this coping style becomes a pattern that interferes with living life, it is called a dissociative disorder.

Splitting takes many forms. Sometimes it works as amnesia. The survivor does not remember significant facts about the trauma. Sometimes survivors will find themselves in places and they have no idea how they got there. Or they are in reality but feel detached from their bodies (flying around the room). People will make jokes "the lights are on but no one is home" because they have no understanding of the process. When there are different realities, sometimes different personalities will form. We call this either *multiple personality disorder* or *dissociative identity disorder.*

Addiction is an important partner to the dissociative process. Psychedelic drugs and marijuana, for example, are hallucinogenic and create an altered reality. Mystical and artistic preoccupation and some forms of excessive religiosity and spiritual practice create altered mental states and can be highly addictive. Two of the features of addictive disorders to sex, food, drugs, gambling and alcohol are preoccupation and obsession. These also have a set of neuropathways that are distinct. Addictions here are called the "fantasy" addictions and often accompany arousal and obsession. Some sex addicts, for example, have a pattern of falling in love. As soon as the romance starts to subside, they find another romance. They live for the thrill and borrow endlessly on the promise of "this is the lover that will make the pain go away."

Another example is the compulsive gambler who buys lottery tickets with the family grocery money and obsesses about winning. He fantasizes endlessly about how he will spend the money he will win and how his profound financial difficulties will be behind him. Sadly, he is not able to face his difficulties because he retreats so often into fantasy that he starts acting as if the fantasy was reality. Similarly, the exhibitionist who is cruising and the alcoholic who becomes the wine connoisseur share the ability to go into a trance about their obsessions; they dissociate from their painful realities.

Addicts will talk of the split in realities by saying they feel like two people: the real person who has values and keeps commitments, and the out-of-control addict whose compulsivity destroys everything important to the "real" person. Robert Louis Stevenson wrote the story of Dr. Jekyll and Mr. Hyde to explain the experience of alcoholism. Addiction and trauma specialists are starting to understand that this *addictive personality shift* is very similar in its processes to multiple personality disorder.

Trauma splitting, then, is ignoring traumatic realities by splitting off the experiences and not integrating them into personality or daily life. Signs of dissociation include:

fantasizing or "spacing out" during plays and movies that generate intense feelings or are reminders of painful experiences

experiencing confusion, absentmindedness and forgetfulness because of preoccupation

living in a fantasy world when things get tough

feeling separate from body as a reaction to a flashback

experiencing amnesia about what you are doing or where you are

being preoccupied with something else than what needs to be attended to

having a life of "compartments" that others do not know
about

living a double life

daydreaming, living in an unreal world

obsessing around addictive behavior

losing yourself in romantic fantasies

the use of marijuana or psychedelic drugs

All of us seek the holodeck at some point in time. The problem starts when we have been hurt so badly that we wish to stay there.

TRAUMA ABSTINENCE

Sandy was an attractive, extremely creative woman who seemed to wind up with dead-end jobs. Her friends wondered about it since she had such wonderful ideas. Her family wondered about it because she worked so hard in school and did so well. Family and friends alike tended to overlook the issue because Sandy was an incest survivor and also a recovering alcoholic. She had one more secret, however. Sandy went to a self-help group for compulsive debtors.

Compulsive debtors are different than compulsive spenders, who are often extremely successful. Spenders find release and escape with purchases. Debtors may buy things, then return them in a cycle similar to the binge/purge cycle of bulimia. Debtors use debt as a form of impoverishment and self-fulfillment. They cannot move or succeed under their debt burden. They have a core belief about their unworthiness.

One night in group the topic was *poverty obsession*. Some group members suggested that Sandy might have this issue. She was incensed. She was so upset she brought it to her therapist. Her therapist responded that she had been thinking the same thing, since she saw a pattern of aversion and self-discipline. Sandy focused so much on denying herself good things that she was self-limiting. Further, her therapist found it amazing that abstaining from alcohol had been so easy for Sandy. It reminded her therapist of compulsive overeaters who switched to being compulsive dieters or who became anorexics. She encouraged Sandy to look at the issue. Sandy was furious with her therapist as well as her group.

At that time Sandy managed a hair salon. In fact, she had created some shampoo and conditioning formulas that her customers loved. Many encouraged her to market the product and build a franchise system, but Sandy did nothing but continue to eke out a living from her shop. One day she was about to shampoo a client when she noticed that she was out of shampoo. Sandy asked one of her employees if she had an open bottle of shampoo. The employee said "sure" but something in her employee's eyes told Sandy that something was amiss. As she proceeded to work with her client she watched her employee from the mirror as she went to the storeroom and came back with a fresh bottle of shampoo. A realization hit Sandy so hard it was as though her emotional breath was taken away. She never went to the storeroom herself. She always "borrowed" an already open bottle of whatever she needed.

Sandy realized she had a pattern of frugality that made it difficult for her to open a new bottle. Her employees would simply go to the storeroom. It was her inventory and her invention, but denying herself was so ingrained in her she had developed the habit of taking open bottles. As it turned out, this frustrated her employees, who regarded their otherwise well-liked supervisor as pretty idiosyncratic. In an instant Sandy realized the significance of the bottle issue. Her whole life was based on control and deprivation until she could no longer stand it, whereupon she would go out of control as in her drinking or spending. This aversion to good, nurturing things for herself was precisely what her therapist and group were trying to tell her. Like all of us, we get most angry at the truths we do not wish to face. Sandy was like many other survivors, who often are extremely creative people. There is something about suffering that enhances creativity. Yet survivors also experience a bottleneck in their lives by their commitment to deprivation.

Compulsive deprivation or abstinence occurs especially around memories of success, high stress, shame or anxiety. Most important, deprivation is driven by terror and fear, which we already know have a powerful impact on our brains. In deprivation survivors may:

deny themselves basic needs like groceries, shoes, books, medical care, rent or heat

avoid any sexual pleasure or feel extreme remorse over any sexual activity

hoard money and avoid spending money on legitimate needs

perform "underachieving" jobs compulsively and make consistently extreme or unwarranted sacrifices for work

spoil success opportunities

have periods of no interest in eating and attempt diets repeatedly

see comfort, luxuries and play activities as frivolous

routinely skip vacations because of dedication to an unrewarding task

avoid normal activities because of fears

have difficulty with play

be underemployed

vomit food or use diuretics to avoid weight gain

While there are many faces to traumatic abstinence, common elements do exist. First is the long shadow of family neglect. Neglectful families teach lessons about self-care and self-esteem. The family environment allows children to become comfortable with deprivation. The neglect of children becomes self-neglect in adults. Couple it with high arousal events such as domestic violence or sexual abuse and you have a neurochemical cocktail that is hard to beat. The antidote to being out of control is to be in supercontrol. Maybe the only way to control survival is to freeze like a hunted animal. Ask nothing. Do nothing. Attract no attention. Yet fear mobilizes the body. Adrenaline, cortisol, endorphins and norepinephrine pour into the body. In a constant state it can become addictive.

All the conditions are there: obsession, profound neurochemical changes and a mechanism to manage the fear. Addiction specialists have long recognized the role of addictive deprivations. Anorexia, or self-starvation, has all the characteristics of drug addiction and is regarded as a fear-based, endorphin-mediated process that can be terminal. Even more important is the role of deprivations in serving as a balance to other excessive out-of-control behaviors. One woman described how when she was out of control sexually she would be anorexic with food. Then she would shut down sexually, become sexually aversive and at the same time become out of control with food. There were one hundred pounds in her life that served to absolutely indicate where she was sexually. Another example is the clergyman who works ninety-five hours a week for an unappreciative congregation, struggling to make ends meet because he is so poorly paid. At the same time he is sexually out of control. It is common among professionals such as members of the clergy, physicians and attorneys to have excessive, out-of-control aspects of their lives rooted in extreme deprivation. The bottom line is: Wherever addiction is, there will also be deprivation. If not addictive in its own right, the deprivation becomes a life pattern that, in part, is a solution to traumatic experience.

TRAUMA SHAME

A little girl is forced to have oral sex with her father. The father then tells her she is a bad little girl for letting this happen and that she is going to go to hell. The child is not sophisticated theologically and can't make sense out of the experience. All she knows is that she is bad and that she will come to a bad end. When the victim feels defective, or even worse, at fault, there is traumatic shame. Shame in this case is a profound sense of unworthiness and self-hatred rooted in traumatic experience.

Shame does not just originate from a perpetrator blaming the victim, although that happens often. Trauma can also leave a feeling of being defective or flawed. Sometimes victims are ashamed of their reactions to trauma—they are no longer like other people. Shame represents a fundamental break in trust. People who become *shame-based* have core beliefs that they are unlovable, that if people knew what they were really like they would leave. They believe there is no hope for change. They do not trust anyone to care about them based on their own merits, especially if the trauma was a significant betrayal by a trusted person.

Survivors will try to compensate by driving themselves to meet unreachable standards in order to gain the acceptance of others. When they fail, they add to their existing shame. An example would be the dieter on a rigorous diet who binges, feels ashamed at the lack of self-discipline, and tries even harder. Addiction specialists see the whole binge/purge phenomenon as rooted in shameful feelings about self. Trauma specialists also note that one of the changes in brain functioning is that all experiences are processed as extremes. Reactions are totally one way or another. There is no mid-ground, which is what also happens with addiction and deprivation. People lose the ability to operate in a balanced way, which further adds to their shameful feelings.

Shame can result in an obsessive self-hatred, which is more than simply feeling unlovable. It is also more than being depressed. It can become a merciless, unforgiving stance with yourself for which the only ultimate solution is suicide. Much time is taken up in thinking about destroying yourself. Another result of shame is self-destructive behavior—doing things that are bound to damage yourself or doing things that would sabotage any success. Clinicians are struck by how victims of trauma, especially in which there is violence, become violent with themselves. Self-mutilation, cutting or hurting themselves and placing themselves in high-risk situations—all are rooted in self-hatred. Even their thought patterns can center upon torturous images of self-inflicted violence.

These signs of shame include:

> feeling ashamed because you believe trauma experiences were your fault
>
> feeling lonely and estranged from others because of trauma experiences
>
> engaging in self-mutilating behaviors (cutting yourself, burning yourself, etc.)
>
> engaging in self-destructive behaviors
>
> enduring physical or emotional pain that most people would not accept
>
> avoiding mistakes "at any cost"
>
> feeling that you should be punished for the trauma event and being unable to forgive yourself
>
> feeling bad when something good happens
>
> having suicidal thoughts, threats and attempts

possessing no ability to experience normal emotions such as sadness, anger, love and happiness

having a deep fear of depending on people

feeling unworthy, unlovable, immoral or sinful because of trauma experiences

perceiving others always as better, happier and more competent

having a dim outlook on the future

avoiding experiences that feel good, have no risk and that are self-nurturing

Consider the story of Ralph, a very successful physician. He learned at an early age to escape his abusive family by being in school. He did not have to be at home as long as he was completely immersed in school activities and was incontestably successful. To outsiders he was the model child. Inside, he lived in emotional shell shock. His father was violent and sexually abusive toward his sisters. In fact, it was Ralph who helped his sisters put locks on their bedroom doors. His efforts to protect his sisters one night resulted in his father badly beating him.

A source of comfort was his mom, who would slip into his bed at night after his dad was asleep in a drunken stupor. He found his mom's body erotic but felt loyalty to his dad. He was confused by his mom's cold demeanor the next day. He never made sense of the cruelty and betrayal he witnessed in his family. He felt embarrassed by his family and empty inside. He compensated by being tops in everything so no one would know his life was a charade. Yet he was troubled by intrusive thoughts of being cut and hurt. Even minor surgery became difficult. The harder he worked, the less life seemed worthwhile. He started drinking heavily and self-prescribed painkillers to numb the pain and postpone the taking of his own life.

Then he became involved with Emily. She was the wife of his best friend, who also was a physician and one of Ralph's partners. Emily was a clinical social worker who clearly was a sex addict. She had a pattern of high-risk sex with many men, although she preferred high-profile professionals. Best of all, she liked the drama if these men knew of each other and sex compromised their professional and personal situations. Her husband knew of her acting out but agreed to it. This reinforced his own feelings of cuckolded shame and gave him permission for his own sexual activities. Ralph became obsessed with Emily and their extraordinary sex. Their whole relationship was a series of broken promises, high drama and painful betrayal. He even found himself getting support from Emily's husband. Ralph knew this relationship was destroying him. He could not work or function, yet he could not leave her. Finally, the state medical board intervened because of his drinking, which had become debilitating. When the board admitted him for treatment, he was absolutely suicidal.

His therapist pointed out to Ralph that he was reexperiencing what had happened to him as a child. He was again part of a group of untrustworthy people of which he was profoundly ashamed. His feelings of unworthiness could not be numbed into submission and, in fact, made him vulnerable to chasing moments of pseudointimacy with a manipulative, exploitive person. Emily was like a drug for him. The only alternative in his desperation and self-hatred was to die. His therapist summed it up when he said, "You have re-created your trauma."

TRAUMA REPETITION

Reenactment. Therapists use the term *repetition compulsion* which means repeating behaviors and/or seeking situations or persons that re-create the trauma experience. Ralph was reliving a story out of his painful history. Some people will find themselves in the same situation, with the same type of person, over and over again in their lives. Yet like Ralph, they may never link their behavior to the original betrayal and trauma. Reenactment is living in the unremembered past.

Connie is a good example. She was raised with an alcoholic father. Like Ralph's dad, Connie's father was very abusive. So it is no surprise that Connie married three abusive alcoholics in a row. The irony is that Connie left each husband to seek a man who would be better. She wanted an upgrade, yet each successive marriage was worse. Connie did change—she changed husbands. The scenario of living with an abusive, hard-drinking man, however, did not change. Each subsequent marriage was a repeat of the first, which was an echo of her childhood experience.

Some survivors repeat not only the same scenario but also the exact behavioral experience. A nurse was hospitalized many times for depression and suicidal feelings. She kept telling people she had this problem with masturbation. Usually this problem was ignored because it was not seen as relevant to her suicidal intentions. Finally, a perceptive therapist explored what the masturbation was really about, and it was not just masturbation. It was autoerotic asphyxiation. She would hang herself in her closet while compulsively masturbating. In her art therapy she drew a picture of her father raping her at the age of ten. In the picture the father is strangling her. What the therapist then learned was the whole story of how when this nurse was a child, her father sexually abused her and then locked her in a closet. So all the elements of the original scenario were there: sexual stimulation, strangulation, extreme danger and the dark closet. She was compulsively reenacting that scene from her childhood. As much as she tried to stop it, she could not. And she was so ashamed, the only way she could ask for help was to be suicidal.

Another form of reenactment is to victimize people in the same way that others victimized you. One incest father related that when he was a kid his parents told him that because he was an uncircumcised child, they needed to stretch his foreskin regularly or he might not be able to be sexual as an adult. This led to the sexual abuse he experienced as a child. As an adult, he reenacted the same abuse with his children. When the grandparents entered therapy, the therapist asked them which doctor had prescribed stimulation of the foreskin. The grandfather responded, "It was not our doctor, it was my father's doctor." This family had received a piece of medical advice in the late 1890s that would become the basis of a sexual abuse history spanning four generations.

Trauma repetition is characterized by:

> doing something self-destructive over and over again, usually something that took place in childhood and started with a trauma
>
> reliving a "story" from the past
>
> engaging in abusive relationships repeatedly
>
> repeating painful experiences, including specific behaviors, scenes, persons and feelings
>
> doing something to others that you experienced as an early life trauma

In part, trauma repetition is an effort by the victim to bring resolution to the traumatic memory. By repeating the experience, the victim tries anew to figure out a way to respond in order to eliminate the fear. Instead, the victim simply deepens the traumatic wound. Note that repetition, like shame, can draw heavily on the other forms of traumatic impact: reactivity, arousal, blocking, splitting and deprivation. Shame and reenactment simply intensify the mind-altering experience of trauma. They become allies of one another. They form a devastating combination when they are part of a trauma bond in which there has been betrayal.

2

TRAUMA BONDS AND THEIR ALLIES

I can't live without him . . . he may beat me, he may cheat me, but I love him. Ain't nobody's business if I do.

PORTER GRAINGER AND EVERETT ROBBINS
"TAIN'T NOBODY'S BIZ-NESS IF I DO"

What do the following people have in common?

Joan was petrified. Her best friend was getting married in a Catholic church. She dreaded anything that would remind her of the priest she had been involved with for eight years. She could hardly stand not being with him, yet being with him was worse, especially when she found out she was one of many. To be in a church again would be agony. Perhaps he could change. Perhaps he would be there.

Fred could not believe it. Here he was doing it again. He was helping his ex-wife—a woman who lied to him for years about her affairs, who attacked him viciously both in and out of the courtroom, who lied to the children, his own

27

family, and friends, and who in typical fashion ignored her own attorney's advice and destroyed the company he built. Yet there was a snow blower he saw on sale, and there was snow on the ground. She had no way of dealing with that in her new house, and it felt good to help her this way. Maybe she will notice.

Because of her abuse history Maxine began therapy. Her therapist, Fran, found out that Maxine was an excellent bookkeeper. Since Fran needed a bookkeeper, Maxine went to work for Fran and also continued in therapy. Maxine discovered that Fran was committing significant Medicare fraud. Fran expected Maxine to cover up the problems because the regulations were so "irrational." Two years after her therapist's indictment and sentencing, Maxine was still troubled by her testifying against Fran.

To belong to Reverend Jim Jones's group was to feel at the same time both deeply cared for and deeply afraid. For all the good that was done, little dissent was tolerated. Even moving out of the country did not help. When Congressman Leo Ryan came to investigate, some decided to leave. All of them were shot trying to escape. The rest committed suicide rather than go against the community. Over 950 people died—out of loyalty.

Jan had a secret. Her dad had been sexual with her since she was nine. She knew it was not right, but she also felt very special. Out of all her sisters, she was picked out. And some nights it felt good. And her mom was such a waste anyway, who could blame him. All the talk about child abuse in health class was disturbing. These people did not understand what it was really like.

These people are all struggling with traumatic bonds. Those standing outside see the obvious. All these relationships are about some insane loyalty or attachment. They share exploitation, fear and danger. They also have elements of kindness, nobility and righteousness. These are all people who stay involved or wish to stay involved with people who betray them. Emotional pain, severe consequences and even the prospect of death do not stop their caring or commitment. Clinicians call this traumatic bonding. This means that the victims have a certain dysfunctional attachment that occurs in the presence of danger, shame or exploitation. There often is seduction, deception or betrayal. There is always some form of danger or risk.

Some relationships are traumatic. Take, for example, the conflictual ties in movies like *The War of the Roses* or *Fatal Attraction*. What Lucy does to Charlie Brown around holding the football every year is a betrayal we have grown to expect. Abuse cycles such as those found in domestic violence are built around trauma bonds. So are the misplaced loyalties found in exploitive cults, incest families, or hostage and kidnapping situations. Codependents who live with alcoholics, compulsive gamblers or sex addicts, and who will not leave no matter what their partners do, may have suffered enough to have a traumatic bond.

Here are signs that trauma bonds exist in your life:

> when you obsess about people who have hurt you and they are long gone (obsess means to be preoccupied, fantasize about and wonder about even though you do not want to)
>
> when you continue to seek contact with people whom you know will cause you further pain
>
> when you go "overboard" to help people who have been destructive to you

when you continue being a "team" member when obviously things are becoming destructive

when you continue attempts to get people who are clearly using you to like you

when you again and again trust people who have proved to be unreliable

when you are unable to distance yourself from unhealthy relationships

when you want to be understood by those who clearly do not care

when you choose to stay in conflict with others when it would cost you nothing to walk away

when you persist in trying to convince people that there is a problem and they are not willing to listen

when you are loyal to people who have betrayed you

when you are attracted to untrustworthy people

when you keep damaging secrets about exploitation or abuse

when you continue contact with an abuser who acknowledges no responsibility

Take Cheryl as an example. Cheryl grew up with a mother who was a compulsive gambler and who supported her addiction by selling sex. The most kind adult in Cheryl's life was a stepfather who eventually left the craziness of living with her mom. But Cheryl always looked for this kindness. What she was exposed to was a series of abusive men. As an adult she had four marriages, each more abusive than the last. She would find men who were kind and brutal. Between marriages she would deprive herself of food, become thin and would sexually binge. When she was married she would compulsively overeat, add seventy pounds and become sexually aversive. In every marriage she was beaten. In this last marriage she was sexually tortured. A neighbor had to call the police and storm the door to get her away from her husband. An astute police chaplain got her into treatment. Cheryl was willing to come because even she could see the pattern was clear.

Here was a professional woman with a master's degree. She was the mother of four children—one with each husband. Even in treatment she looked with horror at what her last husband did one minute and in the next minute would come up with some reason to call him. She would do this even though she could clearly see that any contact with him was dangerous to her. This relationship had become addictive.

TRAUMA BONDS AS ADDICTIVE

How do trauma bonds become addictive? The answer is in the same way other addictions work. The criteria for addiction are the following:

1. Compulsivity: loss of the ability to choose freely whether to stop or continue a behavior
2. Continuation of the behavior despite adverse consequences such as loss of health, job, marriage or freedom
3. Obsession with the behavior

Addicts can clearly know they need to stop and cannot. Despite the consequences they continue high-risk behavior. They become so obsessed with the behavior that all their life priorities—children, work, values, family, hobbies, friends—are sacrificed for the behavior and the preoccupation that goes with it. The addiction becomes a way to escape or obliterate pain. The addict needs the behavior in order to feel normal.

Now reread the previous paragraph and substitute the word *relationship* for the word *behavior*. A working definition of addiction is that it is a pathological relationship with a mood-altering substance or behavior. Addicts grow up not trusting other people. One thing about alcohol, sex, food, gambling and high-risk experiences—they always do what they promise. So, for example, the alcoholic has a relationship with a bottle. In the case of trauma bonds, the relationship itself is mood altering and compelling. This is not about the sadness you would feel over the loss of someone for whom you care. This is about a supercharged relationship that is so compelling it can kill you.

Historically, in traumatic medicine, these relationships have been called trauma bonds. I have called them betrayal bonds because in most circumstances a fundamental betrayal took place. I also call them betrayal bonds because it is helpful for the victim to use the relational term, rather than trauma, which is a clinical term. Using betrayal bond helps the victim gain some clarity about the experience and the nature of the abuse suffered.

There are five realities about these bonds that are very important to know. The first is that trauma bonds are seldom alone. They draw upon the other solutions to trauma we described in chapter 1. Again, Cheryl serves as an example. She had so many betrayals in her life, she was extremely reactive. She used both sex and food to help control her feelings. She used compulsive aversion to both sex and food as a way to balance living in the extremes. She felt incredible shame about her childhood and could escape—or dissociate—from her life with obsession and fantasy about the man who was to make it better. In the spirit of the kind stepfather, this man was to be the solution. Yet she always selected dangerous men who lived on the edge. She simply repeated the childhood scenarios of abuse and betrayal. Trauma bonds are so potent because the other options become like a constellation of allies.

Throughout medical literature on trauma, there are many descriptions of the addictive qualities of trauma, especially as it concerns the bond with the abuser. In the mid-1980s, Johns

Hopkins researcher John Money commented on child victims who continued to put themselves in harm's way or who appeared to precipitate being abused. He observed that such behavior may "signify that the abused has become addicted to abuse: the response to abuse is to stimulate more of it."[1] Similarly, well-known Harvard researcher Bessel van der Kolk carefully reviewed the role of the endogenous opioid system in addiction to the trauma and trauma bonding. He observed:

> *Trauma victims continue to recreate the trauma in some form for themselves, or for others. War veterans may enlist as mercenaries, incest victims may become prostitutes, victims of child physical abuse may provoke subsequent abuse in foster families, victims of child abuse may grow up to become self-mutilators. Still others recreate the trauma by identifying with the aggressor, and perpetuating the same acts on others that were once exercised upon them . . . what these people have in common is a vague sense of apprehension, emptiness, boredom, and anxiety when not involved in activities reminiscent of the trauma.*[2]

Over a decade later we more fully understand the range of options available to people who have trauma bonds. Reactivity, arousal, blocking, splitting, abstinence, shame and repetition compulsion can all be in the service of traumatic bonding. As a result, these supercharged, traumatic relationships can have tremendous power.

The second reality is that trauma bonds and their allies can form a life pattern. Research shows that once you form a trauma bond, you are vulnerable to falling into similar relationships. In Cheryl's case, she had four very similar marriages. They were all men who were kind and abusive. The irony was that when Cheryl left a relationship it was to find a better one. Yet each one was progressively worse. They all started with a romantic glow—the stepfather's kindness. Each then dissolved into abuse and betrayal. The glow returned often enough for Cheryl to remain in the relationship. (Until it was unbearable. Or they left.) They all had that scary intensity that activated the various options Cheryl, as a trauma victim, already had. There was something about the "bad boy" as a grown man that triggered her trauma responses.

In many ways, understanding this reality helps answer the question everyone asks about these situations: "Why doesn't she just leave?" It is not about money. People with many financial options stay in these situations. It is not about being a woman because it happens to men as well. It is not about the person; it becomes a pattern across many relationships. The answer is that she does not leave because she cannot; the chaos, the extreme danger, the living on the edge coupled with a degree of kindness or nobility are all so compelling. She is no different than the alcoholic who cannot leave the bar.

The third reality is that trauma bonds can be very durable bonds. One of the phrases used by clinicians to describe traumatic bonding is the "Stockholm Syndrome." In 1973, a bank robbery occurred in Stockholm in which hostages were taken as a way to force authorities to release some prisoners. The hostage takers were threatening and abusive to their hostages. There were, however, also moments in which they performed little acts of kindness for the hostages. And they presented themselves as having a noble cause. Yet they were also clear that they would kill the hostages if forced to by the authorities. The five-and-a-half-day siege ended with the hostages and hostage takers holed up in the bank vault.

That the captors capitulated was not a surprise. However, what astounded everyone was: (1) the obvious and total cooperation of the hostages; (2) the deep caring the hostages felt for their captors; and (3) the hostage's rage and contempt for those who rescued them. When arrested, the captors left the bank with hugs and kisses and with promises of support, loyalty and care from the hostages. The captors created the right chemistry of loving care alternated with violence, threats and degrading behavior. After serving ten-year prison terms, both hostage takers married woman hostages from the bank. These women knew these men less than a week but were willing, on the basis of their hostage experience, to wait for a decade to commit for a lifetime. All of this was celebrated in a double ceremony attended by many fellow hostages.[3]

The abuse literature is filled with examples of ongoing abuse followed by profound loyalty extending years and decades. There are two interesting characteristics to remember about trauma bonds: They can be formed almost instantaneously, but they can last forever.

The fourth reality is that trauma bonds can happen to anyone. Many readers will remember bank camera film of Patti Hearst who, as "Tanya," willingly helped the Symbionese Liberation Army in a bank holdup. She had been kidnapped, humiliated and repeatedly raped for 18 months. She was an educated and strong-willed descendant of the Hearst family who had totally lost her identity. After her ordeal she immediately married a bodyguard hired by her family to protect her. He was the first strong male she met after her captivity aside from the police officers who rescued her.

Patti Hearst is one of many well-known people of great personal strength who have lost a sense of self in the face of terror and violence: Jozeph Cardinal Mindszenty, who signed false confessions while confined by Hungarian security forces; Judge Giuseppe Digenarro, who was a chief magistrate captured by the Red Brigades; and Dr. Tiede Herrema, who was a United Nations official held by the Irish Republican Army. They are no different in their reports from those who were tortured in Argentina, Ecuador or Iran, or from those interned in concentration camps in Nazi Germany, Russia or China. The dynamics parallel the prostitute who stays with her pimp or the domestic abuse victim who stays with a violent partner. You can be an extremely gifted and strong person with little prior experience with trauma and still, in the context of terror and violence, become traumatically bonded.

There is also a fifth reality about trauma bonds in general: They are not always bad, but they are about survival. Without the betrayal component they may, in fact, be positive. Take, for example, the reunions of military units who have faced combat. Fifty or sixty years later they may still be incredibly close. Going through wartime experiences can forge deep bonds that help people survive. Another example is found in a study of 732 concentration camp survivors who were flown to England at the end of World War II.[4] Today, these survivors still meet annually. The study documents how close they were almost fifty years after the trauma they'd experienced together. A wealth of research shows that in humans, in other primates, and even in other animals, danger and threat deepen attachment. In many circumstances that can be functional. It becomes destructive when people cannot operate in normal circumstances, when it is exploitive and self-destructive and when people cease to make choices for themselves. In short, when it becomes addictive.

TRAUMA BONDS AND THEIR ALLIES: A SELF-ASSESSMENT

It is important to take stock of what you have learned so far. One way to do that is to see what impact trauma has had on your life. What follows is a series of questions to help you clarify your thinking about your own behavior. There are 144 questions, and it will take approximately forty to sixty minutes to complete them and the accompanying worksheets. Many have found this inventory to be extremely helpful in understanding their behavior. I have placed the inventory here in this chapter because having the results in mind at this early point will help you think about the chapters that follow. Plus, later on in the book we will use the results of this inventory in preparing a recovery plan. I strongly encourage you to take the time to complete the inventory.

Post-Traumatic Stress Index

The following statements typify reactions trauma victims often have to child abuse. Please check those you believe apply to you. Although the statements are written in the present tense, if the statements have *ever* applied to your life, then place a check next to that item. Statements are considered false only if they have *never* been a part of your life. If in doubt, let your first reaction be your guide. Given these guidelines, place a check mark next to the statements you feel apply.

_____ 1. I have recurring memories of painful experiences.
_____ 2. I am unable to stop a harmful childhood pattern.
_____ 3. I sometimes obsess about people who have hurt me and are now gone.
_____ 4. I feel bad at times about myself because of shameful experiences I believe were my fault.
_____ 5. I am a risk taker.
_____ 6. At times, I have difficulty staying awake.
_____ 7. I sometimes feel separate from my body as a reaction to a flashback or memory.
_____ 8. I deny myself basic needs at times, like groceries, shoes, books, medical care, rent and heat.
_____ 9. I have distressing dreams about experiences.
_____10. I repeat painful experiences over and over.
_____11. I try to be understood by those who are incapable or don't care for me.
_____12. I have suicidal thoughts.
_____13. I engage in high-risk behaviors.
_____14. I eat excessively to avoid problems.
_____15. I avoid thoughts or feelings associated with my trauma experiences.
_____16. I skip vacations because of lack of time or money.

____17. I have periods of sleeplessness.

____18. I try to re-create an early trauma experience.

____19. I keep secrets for people who have hurt me.

____20. I have attempted suicide.

____21. I am sexual when frightened.

____22. I drink to excess when life is too hard.

____23. I avoid stories, parts of movies or reminders of early painful experiences.

____24. I avoid sexual pleasure.

____25. I sometimes feel like an old painful experience is happening now.

____26. There is something destructive I do over and over from my early life.

____27. I stayed in conflict with someone when I could have walked away.

____28. I have suicidal thoughts.

____29. I often feel sexual when I am lonely.

____30. I use depressant drugs as a way to cope.

____31. I am unable to recall important details of painful experiences.

____32. I avoid doing "normal" activities because of fears I have.

____33. I have sudden, vivid or distracting memories of painful experiences.

____34. I attempt to stop activities I know are not helpful.

____35. I go overboard to help people who have been destructive.

____36. I often feel lonely and estranged from others because of painful experiences I have had.

____37. I feel intensely sexual when violence occurs.

____38. My procrastinating interferes with my life activities.

____39. I sometimes withdraw or have no interest in important activities because of childhood experiences.

____40. I will hoard money and not spend money on legitimate needs.

___41. I am upset when there are reminders of abusive experiences like anniversaries, places or symbols.

___42. I compulsively do things to others that were done to me as a young person.

___43. I sometimes help those who continue to harm me.

___44. I feel unable to experience certain emotions (love, happiness, sadness, etc.).

___45. I feel sexual when degraded or used.

___46. Sleep is a way for me to avoid life's problems.

___47. I have difficulty concentrating.

___48. I have attempted diets repeatedly.

___49. I have difficulty sleeping.

___50. My relationships are the same story over and over.

___51. I feel loyal to people even though they have betrayed me.

___52. I have a dim outlook on my future.

___53. I feel sexual when someone is "nice" to me.

___54. At times I am preoccupied with food and eating.

___55. I experience confusion often.

___56. I refuse to buy things even when I need them and have the money.

___57. I have difficulty feeling sexual.

___58. I know that something destructive I do repeats a childhood event.

___59. I remain a "team" member when obviously things are becoming destructive.

___60. I feel as if I must avoid depending on people.

___61. I sometimes feel bad because I enjoyed experiences that were exploitive of me.

___62. I abuse alcohol often.

___63. I tend to be accident-prone.

___64. I spend much time performing underachieving jobs.

___65. Sometimes I have outbursts of anger or irritability.

___66. I do things to others that were done to me in my family.

___67. I make repeated efforts to convince people who were destructive to me and not willing to listen.

___68. I engage in self-destructive behaviors.

___69. I get "high" on activities that are dangerous to me.

___70. I use TV, reading and hobbies as ways to numb out.

___71. I go into a fantasy world when things are tough.

___72. I am underemployed.

___73. I am extremely cautious of my surroundings.

___74. I have thoughts and behaviors repeatedly that do not feel good to me.

___75. I attempt to be liked by people who clearly are exploiting me.

___76. I engage in self-mutilating behaviors (cutting self, burning, bruising, etc.).

___77. I use drugs like cocaine or amphetamines to speed things up

___78. I put off certain tasks.

___79. I use "romance" as a way to avoid problems.

___80. I feel very guilty about any sexual activity.

___81. I often feel that people are out to take advantage of me.

___82. I revert to doing things I did as a child.

___83. I am attracted to untrustworthy people.

___84. I endure physical or emotional pain most people would not accept.

___85. I like "living on the edge" of danger or excitement.

___86. When things are difficult, I will sometimes binge.

___87. I have a tendency to be preoccupied with something other than what I need to be.

___88. I have a low interest in sexual activity.

___89. I am distrustful of others.

___90. Some of my recurring behavior comes from early life experiences.

___91. I trust people who have proved to be unreliable.

___92. I try to be perfect.

____ 93. I am orgasmic when hurt or beaten.

____ 94. I use drugs to escape.

____ 95. I use marijuana or psychedelics to hallucinate.

____ 96. I sometimes spoil success opportunities.

____ 97. I am startled more easily than others.

____ 98. I am preoccupied with children of a certain age.

____ 99. I seek people whom I know will cause me pain.

____100. I avoid mistakes at any cost.

____101. I love to gamble on outcomes.

____102. I work too hard so I won't have to feel.

____103. I will often lose myself in fantasies rather than deal with real life.

____104. I go without necessities for periods of time.

____105. I get physical reactions to reminders of abuse experiences (breaking out in cold sweat, trouble breathing, etc.).

____106. I engage in abusive relationships repeatedly.

____107. I have difficulty distancing myself from unhealthy relationships.

____108. I sometimes want to hurt myself physically.

____109. I need lots of stimulation so I will not be bored.

____110. I get "lost" in my work.

____111. I live a "double life."

____112. I vomit food or use diuretics to avoid weight gain.

____113. I feel anxious about being sexual.

____114. There is a certain age of children or adolescents that is sexually attractive to me.

____115. I continue to have contact with a person who has abused me.

____116. I often feel unworthy, unlovable, immoral or sinful because of experiences I have had.

____117. I like sex when it is dangerous.

____118. I try to "slow down" my mind.

____119. I like "compartments" that others do not know about.

___120. I experience periods when I'm not interested in eating.

___121. I am scared about sex.

___122. There are activities that I have trouble stopping even though they are useless or destructive.

___123. I am in emotional fights (divorces, lawsuits) that seem endless.

___124. I often feel I should be punished for past behavior.

___125. I do sexual things that are risky.

___126. When I am anxious, I will do things to stop my feelings.

___127. I have a fantasy life that I retreat to when things are hard.

___128. I have difficulty with play.

___129. I wake up with upsetting dreams.

___130. My relationships seem to have the same dysfunctional pattern.

___131. There are certain people whom I always allow to take advantage of me.

___132. I have a sense that others are always better off than me.

___133. I use cocaine or amphetamines to heighten high-risk activities.

___134. I don't tolerate uncomfortable feelings.

___135. I am a daydreamer.

___136. At times, I see comfort, luxuries and play activities as frivolous.

___137. I hate it when someone approaches me sexually.

___138. Sometimes I find children more attractive than others.

___139. There are some people in my life who are hard to get over, though they hurt or used me badly.

___140. I feel bad when something good happens.

___141. I get excited/aroused when faced with dangerous situations.

___142. I use anything to distract myself from my problems.

___143. Sometimes I live in an "unreal" world.

___144. There are long periods of time with no sexual activity for me.

Traumatic Stress Index Answer Sheet

Place an *X* next to all statements that are true about you. Add up all the *X*s in each column and place the total in the space at the bottom of each column.

1.___	2.___	3.___	4.___	5.___	6.___	7.___	8.___
9.___	10.___	11.___	12.___	13.___	14.___	15.___	16.___
17.___	18.___	19.___	20.___	21.___	22.___	23.___	24.___
25.___	26.___	27.___	28.___	29.___	30.___	31.___	32.___
33.___	34.___	35.___	36.___	37.___	38.___	39.___	40.___
41.___	42.___	43.___	44.___	45.___	46.___	47.___	48.___
49.___	50.___	51.___	52.___	53.___	54.___	55.___	56.___
57.___	58.___	59.___	60.___	61.___	62.___	63.___	64.___
65.___	66.___	67.___	68.___	69.___	70.___	71.___	72.___
73.___	74.___	75.___	76.___	77.___	78.___	79.___	80.___
81.___	82.___	83.___	84.___	85.___	86.___	87.___	88.___
89.___	90.___	91.___	92.___	93.___	94.___	95.___	96.___
97.___	98.___	99.___	100.___	101.___	102.___	103.___	104.___
105.___	106.___	107.___	108.___	109.___	110.___	111.___	112.___
113.___	114.___	115.___	116.___	117.___	118.___	119.___	120.___
121.___	122.___	123.___	124.___	125.___	126.___	127.___	128.___
129.___	130.___	131.___	132.___	133.___	134.___	135.___	136.___
137.___	138.___	139.___	140.___	141.___	142.___	143.___	144.___

TRT___ TR___ TBD___ TS___ TP___ TB___ TSG___ TA___

Traumatic Stress Index Worksheet

Match your scores with the appropriate capitalized code. Behind each score is an explanation of what the score measures. Also included are some recommendations for actions that would be appropriate for you to take. If your score is low (0–3), this is not an area of concern for you. If your score is moderate (3–6), you should discuss with friends or a therapist what strategies would now help you. If your score is higher than six, this should be an area of intense focus for you. You may wish to discuss with a therapist a series of target activities to help you with these trauma patterns. Remember, this is only a paper and pencil instrument to help you think about the role of trauma in your life. Only you and your therapist can see if the results fit your experience.

SCORE	CHARACTERISTICS	THERAPY STRATEGIES
TRT _____	TRAUMA REACTIONS: Experiencing current reactions to trauma events in the past	Study ways you are still reacting. Write letters to your perpetrators telling them of the long-term impact you are experiencing. Also write amends letters to those you know you have harmed. Decide with therapist what is appropriate to send.
TR _____	TRAUMA REPETITION: Repeating behaviors or situations that parallel early trauma experiences	Understand how history repeats itself in your life experiences. Develop habits that help to center yourself (e.g. breathing, journaling), so that you are doing what you intend, not the cycles of old. Work on boundaries. Boundary failure is key to repetition compulsion.

TBD _____	TRAUMA BONDS: Being connected (loyal, helpful, supportive) to people who are dangerous, shaming or exploitive	Learn to recognize trauma bonds by identifying those in your life. Look for patterns. Use "detachment" strategies for difficult people. Use a First Step if necessary.
TS _____	TRAUMA SHAME: Feeling unworthy and having self-hate because of trauma experience	Understand the shame dynamics of your family. Why was it important to you that you feel shameful? Start reprogramming yourself with affirmations.
TP _____	TRAUMA PLEASURE: Finding pleasure in the presence of extreme danger, violence, risk or shame	Do a history of how excitement and shame are hooked up to your trauma past. Note the costs and dangers to you over time. Do a First Step and relapse-prevention plan about how powerful this is in your life.
TB _____	TRAUMA BLOCKING: A pattern exists to numb, block out or overwhelm feelings that stem from trauma in your life	Work to identify experiences that caused pain or diminished you. Reexperience feelings and make sense of them with help. This will reduce the power they have had. Do a First Step if appropriate.
TSG _____	TRAUMA SPLITTING: Ignoring traumatic realities by dissociating or "splitting" off experiences or parts of self	Learn that dissociating is a "normal" response to trauma. Identify ways you split reality and the triggers that cause that to happen. Cultivate a caring adult who stays present so you can stay whole. Notice any powerlessness you feel.
TA _____	TRAUMA ABSTINENCE: Depriving yourself of things you need or deserve because of traumatic acts	Understand how deprivation is a way to continue serving your perpetrators. Write a letter to the victim that was you about learning to tolerate pain and deprivation. Work on strategies to self-nurture, including inner-child visualizations.

For most people, completing the Traumatic Stress Index provides much to think about. First of all, you may have noticed patterns that were clear to you before. This will help lay the groundwork for change. Sometimes people are anxious because they scored high on some of the scales. Take comfort in knowing that you have identified where some of the issues are. Pinpointing the problem means you can take the action your worksheet suggested.

Perhaps you disagree with the results. Or maybe nothing significant or new emerged. That sometimes happens. Remember, this was only a paper and pencil exercise to help give you clarity. It may not have been a good match for your experiences. I encourage you to keep reading, however. What is important is to understand what trauma can do to you. In the next chapter we take the next step by examining what betrayal does to relationships.

3

WHAT DOES BETRAYAL
DO TO RELATIONSHIPS?

*Anyone who hasn't experienced the ecstasy of betrayal
knows nothing about ecstasy at all.*

JEAN GENET, *PRISONER OF LOVE*

It happens every fall. Lucy Van Pelt offers to hold the
football for Charlie Brown. Every time this happens, Charlie
Brown recognizes that this is a ploy to use him. And every
time, Lucy comes up with a plausible reason why Charlie
Brown should trust her. Charlie Brown sets aside his distrust
and takes a risk again. Lucy then does what she always does—
jerks the football out of the way at the last second. Charlie
Brown always ends up flat on his back. Lucy then makes it
clear why he should not have trusted her. We smile because
the scenario is so familiar and perverse it is comical. It also
contains the basic elements of deception and seduction that
are the essence of betrayal.

In real life the scenario ceases to be funny. Here are some
examples:

A nationally known physician is approached by a hospital administrator about setting up a program in his specialty. Meetings are held with staff to prepare a proposal for the board of directors. The physician is promised the medical director's position for the program. The proposal is turned down by the board but the administrator encourages another round of breakfast meetings and work sessions. Again the proposal is turned down, followed by more meetings. The physician starts to distrust the process and drops out of the planning. Six months later the program opens. A staff member confides to the physician that the administrator never intended to use the physician but needed his expertise to train staff and put the program together. The board had never seen the proposal. The administrator simply used the physician with no intention of ever hiring him. When challenged, the administrator says the physician lost hope too early. The staff says this is the administrator's common method for getting "free" consultation.

A rabbi sets up a special religious education course for adolescent girls. Parents are thrilled with the prospect. Part of the new curriculum involves sex education, however, and some parents withdraw their children because of rumors of the rabbi being "too close" to some of the girls. Other parents steadfastly keep their daughters enrolled. They write the rumors off to temple politics and the sexual rigidity of some of the parents. Nobody in the congregation is prepared for the revelations that the beloved rabbi is, in fact, having sex with a number of the girls in a sex ring.

Carol is a woman in her early forties. She is an investment broker married to a wealthy CEO with his own company. Together they have raised three daughters, all in their early twenties. Carol starts a passionate affair with a man whose source of money is difficult to determine. But the passion is in sharp contrast to the "lifeless" marriage she sees herself in. Her sexual experiences with her new partner are unlike anything she's experienced with her spouse. She leaves her husband amidst much anguish from her daughters and a lot of anger from him. Once living with her new partner, the nightmare begins—beatings and torture to the extent of being hospitalized twice. He is so in control of her life she cannot go to the bathroom by herself. One day while sitting in my office, and after being pulled out of her nightmare, I ask her why she stayed with this man. Her answer comes from some distant place inside: "The sex was good."

In each example there is a promise. In the physician's case, it was the professional position and recognition he always wanted. In the rabbi's case, it was the promise of a solid religious education that had solid parental support. For Carol, it was a form of sexual redemption that would pull her out of a sterile, emotionless marriage. Common to all was a promise. Those who betray read their victims well. They appeal to the emptiness, the unfinished and the wounds of others. The promise is designed to fix, to heal, to resolve or to make up for what has happened.

The promise is so appealing that intuitions are set aside. Even Charlie Brown knows better. In the cartoon on the following page, Charlie Brown sets his suspicions aside because Lucy sounds sincere. He wants to believe so badly that Lucy will hold the football that he persuades himself to take yet another run at it. The promise and his desire to believe the promise are so great that he ignores the obvious and accepts the improbable. And once again, he is sucked back into the inevitable result.

There are five main ways promises are used to betray. They are: betrayal by seduction, betrayal by terror, betrayal by exploitation of power, betrayal by intimacy and betrayal by spirit. One of these is bad enough, but oftentimes all five are present. To understand traumatic bonding, the reader must understand these separate types of abuse. We start with betrayal by seduction.

BETRAYAL BY SEDUCTION

Seduction is high warmth with low intention. For example, if a person touches your arm during a conversation, it may simply be a gesture of human kindness. It also could be considered warm and connecting. However, the same touch could also be a sexual overture. If the intention is not clear, you may not know what the touch means. Lack of intention can cover risk. If the person who touched you was indeed testing for sexual interest, when challenged as to what he wanted, the person could say, "Oh, I was just being friendly." So communicating and understanding personal intent are incredibly important skills that must be learned.

Figure 3.1 graphically creates contrasts between high and low warmth and between high and low intention. What emerges from these contrasts are four possible combinations.

First there is high warmth and high intention. This can be a very close and rewarding relationship because you know where you stand with a person who wants to be connected with you. Characteristics of this combination are:

> relationships are committed and involved
>
> agreements are clear and rewarding
>
> feelings are excited and enthusiastic
>
> trust is high
>
> rewards are immediate or concrete
>
> risk is mutually shared

Figure 3.1. Warmth and Intention

WARMTH

		HIGH	LOW
I N T E N T I O N	**H I G H**	relationships are committed and involved	relationships are goal-oriented rather than people-oriented
		feelings are excited and enthusiastic	agreements are clear but disconnected or unemotional
		agreements are clear and rewarding	feelings are disconnected or unemotional
		trust is high	trustworthy
		rewards are immediate or concrete	rewards are specified and reliable
		risk is mutually shared	risk is minimal
	L O W	relationships are manipulative and exploitive	relationships are inscrutable and disengaged
		agreements are ill-defined, unclear or tentative	agreements are short-term and difficult to negotiate
		feelings are anxious and intense	feelings are absent
		trust depends often on exaggerated or unreal promises	high distrust
		rewards are in the future and often conditional	rewards are minimal
		risk is often one-sided	no risk since little is asked

The second is low warmth and high intention. These are very task-centered relationships in which the primary objective is to accomplish a transaction or do a job. It is simple and businesslike. We all have such relationships because they are very functional. Characteristics of this combination are:

relationships are goal-oriented rather than people-oriented

agreements are clear but emotionally detached

feelings are disconnected or unemotional

trustworthiness

rewards are specified and reliable

risk is minimal

The third is high warmth with low intention. These relationships are very deceptive and seductive, and commonly found in traumatic bonding. If the person was clear about his intention, the other might not respond or become involved. Characteristics of this combination are:

relationships are manipulative and exploitive

agreements are ill-defined, unclear or tentative

feelings are anxious and intense

trust depends often on exaggerated or unreal promises

rewards are in the future and often conditional

risk is often one-sided

The fourth combination is low intention and low warmth. These are difficult relationships because there seems to be no obvious purpose for them. It is not about human contact or any specific desire. Characteristics of this combination are:

relationships are inscrutable and disengaged

agreements are short-term and difficult to negotiate

feelings are absent

high distrust

rewards are minimal

no risk since little is asked

The high warmth/low intention combination is often found in betrayal scenarios. The emotional content of the relationship obscures what the partner's true intent is. Warmth can be expressed in many ways:

    expression of admiration and liking

    expression of caring and concern

    indication of long-term relationship

    affectionate gestures and touching

    positive, upbeat conversation about the relationship, project or challenge at hand

    excitement, and desire to get to know you better

    complimenting and fawning behavior

    excessive familiarity

    personal revelations and disclosures that may feel inappropriate to the context

But if the real agenda is not expressed, it may be seduction. When the warmth is part of an effort to get you to do something and it is obvious, you distrust it. When the politician seeking your vote or the car salesman pushing a car uses too much warmth, we use words like *sleaze* or *smooth* because we do not like being finessed or manipulated.

People who come from dysfunctional families in which there was abuse or trauma are particularly vulnerable to seduction. First, because of the intrusion that is part of living in exploitive systems the boundaries that prevent most people from being deceived are not there. These people have not been taken care of or protected, so they may not know how to protect or care for themselves. Most of us learn not to be easily conned into things that might hurt us. Trauma survivors can be extremely naive even while being vigilant. Their discernment and common sense have been impaired by living with secrets, denial, deception and exploitation.

Further, they are vulnerable because of the nature of traumatic shame. The nature of shame creates disconnection with the self and often results in doubting your own perceptions. When a person feels flawed and unlovable, flattery, attention and kindness can further disarm any concerns. When flattered or fawned over, the person will ignore that voice within that says, "Don't do this." Anybody can be seduced. But if you are shameful, needy and afraid, you are much more easily led down the trail of exploitation.

Some survivors continually are attracted to people who were like their abusers, people who can re-create the same situations over and over again. These people can reseduce them repeatedly because the attraction is so powerful. The phrase sometimes used in treatment is that "the picker is broken." Translation? A person will invariably seek out people who will do them harm or betray them. Healthy people with integrity and appropriate boundaries are boring. There is no adrenaline rush, no phenylethyliamine high (the key chemical in "falling in love"), nor is there the mobilization of the endocrine system to cope with crisis.[1] Jack McGinnes, one of the chaplains at The Meadows, wrote a Country-Western song that captures this process well. When he sings it, there is laughter and shouts of self-recognition. One of the frequent lines is "if you won't leave me I will find someone who will." And the song's refrain is "I am just addicted to emotional pain."

Along with the seduction comes a sustaining fantasy or supportive script. The victim of seduction usually wants so badly for the story to be true that she will overlook the obvious and accept the improbable. The sustaining fantasy can come in a number of forms:

> The belief in the story: There usually is a tale that explains why we are in the situation we are in, why we are taking specific actions or where we are headed.

The belief in the person: The abuser, who may be doing wonderful things for others, is viewed as someone with high credibility whose behavior is beyond question.

The belief in the dream: Almost always there is the promise of realizing some cherished goal, be it a personal goal, a state of well-being or the redressing of some loss or wound.

The belief in the mission: Often there is some noble cause or meaningful vision that requires personal sacrifice.

Whatever the script, the victim of betrayal wants to believe it so badly that common sense is abandoned. I know a counselor who made this point in family week very effectively. In a lecture on self-care, she described how she went about buying a new car, a new "vette." The next day she gave a lecture in which she mentioned that a family member of hers used her "Chevette." Of course, everyone had thought she had bought a new Corvette. She challenged the audience as to why they thought she was driving a brand new red Corvette when she had only said "vette." Family week participants always reply that they wanted her to have a nice, expensive sports car. Then, with a penetrating stare, she tells them that they wanted to believe the story so much that they automatically put her in the Corvette. Then when she asks if anyone has bought a vette lately, there is stunned silence. Everyone knows what she means. Everyone had wanted to believe the addicts in their families so much they would make leaps to believe their stories, even when they were not true.

To put it another way, Charlie Brown wanted so badly to kick the football, he would misperceive Lucy as sincere when she was not. There will always be the look of sincerity. Seduction always relies on the victim's willingness to trust again. In betrayal bonds, the victim prefers the story over facts, behaviors and results.

BETRAYAL BY TERROR

If you cannot achieve your goals by seduction, there is always terror. Logic would say that using fear and threat is not a good way to gain cooperation or loyalty. The irony is that in a perverse way it is. Fear immobilizes and deepens attachment. It escalates attraction and arousal. It provides addictive intensity and obsession. It keeps behavior secret. And it is very flexible and can be applied in a variety of situations at varying levels:

> the incest daughter who is told that if she says anything, the family will be destroyed and Dad and Mom will go to jail

> the corporation that retaliates viciously to any employee who raises issues and therefore keeps a tight lid on sexual harassment problems

> the wife who knows in her heart that her husband is right about the fact that he will always be able to find her and kill her

> the child of the raging alcoholic who walks on eggshells because he knows that the next out-of-control rage could be deadly

> the client who is told by her therapist that unless she complies and continues therapy, the therapist will have to reveal their sexual activities to her extremely jealous, abusive husband

> the wife of the physician who has four children and is told she cannot reveal what she knows because her husband would lose his license and there would be no money to support her

Terror works better when coupled with seduction. Even in concentration camps, prisoners who were tortured often experienced a "good cop, bad cop" strategy. False confessions are more likely when there is someone who talks kindly and seems to have some compassion for the prisoner. We have already noted how acts of kindness create traumatic bonding in hostage situations. If the seduction has a powerful story line, the terror can be excused and actually bring people together. The incest daughter might believe the story about Mom's treatment of Dad. Or the client of the therapist might believe him to be the heroic helper of others who was trapped in marriage with a shrew of a wife. Or the hostage might develop sympathy for a rebel with a good cause. If the story is strong enough and well told, the victim of terror can also believe that she or he deserves it, created it, has to endure it and is part of it.

The classic combination of seduction and terror is used very successfully by modern cults. Studies of organized cults have received national attention because they revealed recruitment processes that are often well organized, well funded campaigns built on the twin principles of seduction and terror. They are marketing campaigns that hide behind kindness and opportunity. They offer financial success, happiness, self-fulfillment and instant family or friends. They come in the form of stress seminars, business opportunities, study groups and personal growth groups. What lurks behind this curtain of positive activities is an organization that will take over someone's life, exploit the person's resources and energy, and demand an exacting discipline with little tolerance for deviation.

Consider the story of a Texas group whose leader was a woman who promised adolescent girls she could make them into championship horseback riders. She appealed to their love of horses. What they got, however, was day after day of hard physical labor and religious study that was so abusive, police intervened. Or look at the Heaven's Gate cult in Southern California, which ended with thirty-nine suicides. Here you had a charismatic leader, Marshall Applewhite, who at one time in his life was arrested for sexual misconduct but ended his life castrated along with his most devoted followers. (Note the themes of high arousal and traumatic abstinence.) Heaven's Gate was seen by cult specialists as "mainstream" in its outreach campaign. The cult targeted college campuses and appealed to young people who liked computers.[2]

One of the most successful strategies used by cults is the *love bomb*. When a new member joins a group the person is lavished with praise and attention. Members of the group offer to study with the new member, spend social time, share meals and spend holidays together. It is an instant community of friends so intensely rewarding it feels like the "family you always wanted." But when new members raise a question about their loyalty, they quickly feel the withdrawal of support. If emotionally impoverished or from a dysfunctional family, there is the terror of abandonment. They find that the "family they always wanted" exacts a huge price. Sometimes the penance for wrongdoing is harsh (i.e., long hours of work, extra efforts to recruit other members or sexual favors). This is a convenient way to introduce exploitation and make the member feel responsible.

The love bomb is a great way to enforce group discipline and keep it closed from outsiders who raise disturbing questions (e.g., family members, therapists, media and police). The love bomb strategy can work in a wide variety of contexts. Victims of domestic abuse describe the initial courtship in love bomb terms. Similar stories are told by incest victims.

If the story is strong enough and there is sufficient terror, the outcome is also guilt and shame. Clear evidence for that can be found in how reluctant victims are to report offenses. For example, 50 percent of women living in North America will experience sexual assault sometime in their lives. Much of the time it will be by people that they know. Only 7 percent of those assaulted women will report the offense. Seduction, shame and self-doubt erode whatever sense of self the person had.[3] The combination of seduction and fear is a potent combination used to distort personal judgment. One of the best platforms for exploiting this relationship chemistry is power.

BETRAYAL BY POWER

It was a story more fitting for the front page of a tabloid than the *Wall Street Journal.* The company was the American division of a huge international pharmaceutical corporation. It was the successful manufacturer of the second largest selling drug in the world. *Business Week* broke the scandal. Older women (past forty) were systematically removed and replaced by young, extremely attractive single women. These women were recruited for sex and harassed brutally by the top four executives of the firm. There was also the small problem of the embezzlement of millions of dollars. The result was that the parent company had to make a huge settlement for sexual harassment.

Other victims of sexual harassment do not fare as well. A major airline received complaints of sexual harassment in its Boston office. The woman complaining was a baggage handler. She reported to company officials that after filing the complaint, her life was threatened. The company did not respond. She reported more threats. Finally, the woman was found brutally murdered in the trunk of her car. The company spokesman defended the company, saying there was little they could do.

Sexual harassment is a widespread problem affecting 42 percent of women and 15 percent of men in occupational settings.[4] Movies like *Disclosure, Fatal Attraction* and *Presumed Innocent* reflect our growing concern and consciousness toward the issue. The Pentagon has already spent in excess of a billion dollars resolving sexual harassment issues in the military.

Yet only 1 to 7 percent of sexual harassment victims ever

report the crime. There are many reasons for this, but primary is the disequilibrium of power.[5] One of the most famous cases is Anita Hill's complaint about Clarence Thomas when he was being considered for his position on the Supreme Court. One of the many hotly debated questions was why Anita Hill waited so long to report her experience. Some point to the reality that the only person to report the harassment to was the head of the EEOC, Clarence Thomas. Perhaps there is another explanation—traumatic bonding. You can see it in other forms of abuse involving the disequilibrium of power. Take incest, for example. DeYoung and Lowry define trauma bonding as:

> *the evolution of emotional dependency between two persons of unequal power—an adult and a child, within a relationship characterized by periodic sexual abuse. The nature of this bond is distinguished by feelings of intense attachment, cognitive distortions, and behavioral strategies of both individuals that paradoxically strengthen and maintain the bond.*[6]

Incest survivors may also wait years to report what happened. What incest and sexual harassment have in common is the exploitation by people in power of those most vulnerable to them. If you're not equal in power, then by definition you're vulnerable. And that vulnerability is critical to trauma bonding. The misuse of power, which includes terror and seduction, induces fear, anxiety and self-doubt—all critical aspects of traumatic reactivity.

Here is how it works. Take the example of the executive director of a social service agency who starts an affair with one of his three department heads. Both are married, so there is lots of fear and secrecy. The department head feels very special but also very precarious. She receives special treatment. In return, she tells her secret partner what the other department heads really say about him. He cannot go to them and acknowledge where or how he heard about their opinions, but he starts treating them differently. The other department heads start to doubt their own perceptions and feel fear. Soon the whole organization feels crazy. The department head involved with her boss no longer can separate her performance from their relationship. Is she well-treated because she is a willing employee or a willing bed partner?

To go one more step, add a further level of authority. The executive director now has an affair with a counselor who works for the department head who reports to the director. All the above conditions are made worse. The counselor feels even more precarious and protective than a department head would. In pillow talk the counselor tells the director how the staff perceive each of the department heads. And so now the organization is even more anxious. Figure 3.2 depicts four levels of the social service agency, starting with the board on top and counseling clients on the bottom. The more levels of authority crossed, the more problems there are. The worst-case scenario would be if a member of the board of directors was involved with a client being seen by a counselor.

Figure 3.2. Organizational Incest—I

Board Members	XXXXX
Executive Director	X
Supervisors	XXX
	XXX
	XXX
	XXX
	XXX
Staff	XXX
	XXX
	XXX
	XXX
	XXX
Clients	XXX

Organizational incest is no different from incest in the family, which in reality is no different from sexual misconduct by clergy or health professionals, which is no different from the abuse of physical power in date rape or domestic abuse. They all take advantage of the vulnerable, and they all can result in the dysfunctional attachments we call trauma bonds.[7]

BETRAYAL BY INTIMACY

I was in a large city conducting a workshop. During my stay I was invited to sign books at a bookstore within a large clinic. I was familiar with the clinic's program since the staff had referred a patient to me. I looked forward to meeting the staff and talking about the patient's progress. The book signing went well and the staff were very engaging, but at the end of a long day I was ready to go back to my hotel. The clinic manager offered to drive me back. We got into the car, and as we were about to leave the parking lot, she burst into tears, pounded her fists on the steering wheel, and said between clenched teeth and tears, "I can't let him do this to you!"

Haltingly and between sobs the story poured out. Her husband was the doctor who owned the clinic. She was his fifth wife. He was charming and very engaging during the first year of their marriage. Then one day, one of the male staff members walked into her husband's office to return a book to his library and found him having sexual intercourse with a woman client. When his wife found out, she was furious and promptly moved out. She then told me that in the six months since this all took place, he had two other young women in their early twenties as lovers. He was in his late fifties.

I interrupted her and asked if anyone had reported him. She said no. I asked why she hadn't. Her story went like this: When she discovered he was sleeping with patients, she immediately asked for a divorce. In dividing up the property, she found he had not paid employment taxes to the IRS for the entire clinic for three years. She knew the IRS to be unforgiving about this type of situation. If you are married to someone who has not paid taxes, you are liable for half. She knew she could not make that amount of money. So she became the clinic manager and started to aggressively pay back the taxes. She concluded that in about four months, all the taxes would be paid and then she could report him and divorce him. I asked if she knew if he was still having sex with his patients, and she said that it was probably happening.

I stayed over an extra day and met individually with staff members. If they did not report him, I would have to do it. Every person I talked with knew about the problem but was in some incredible bind with this doctor. For example, there was a single-parent mom who was completing her supervised hours for her clinical internship. She was desperate to finish so that she could support her children. She knew that if he was reported, she would have to do the internship all over and go through an additional twelve months of agony. She could not do it to her children. Then there was the counselor who made the initial discovery. He owed the doctor substantial amounts of money. There was also the best friend whom he black-mailed. Everyone had a story. To their credit, they banded together and reported the doctor.

The binds they were in are familiar. In addition to a betrayal by power, you had a betrayal of intimacy. Whatever vulnerability existed, the doctor exploited. His wife and friend were betrayed by their trust. Those who worked for him clinically were betrayed by his power.

To return to our graphic of the hypothetical social service agency, in figure 3.3 I have added, in addition to levels of power, the intimate partners of those at each level. Thus the executive director could have an affair with the spouse of one of the supervisors who worked for him. Both power and intimacy would be betrayed in that scenario. The doctor in the agency I visited had essentially done both as well.

There is only one thing worse than someone who betrays using seduction, terror, power and intimacy: someone who betrays by the spirit.

Figure 3.3. Organizational Incest—II

	STAFF	PARTNERS
Board Members	XXXXX	OOOOO
Executive Director	X	O
Supervisors	XXX	OOO
Staff	XXX	OOO
	XXX	OOO
	XXX	OOO
	XXX	OOO
	XXX	OOO
	XXX	OOO
	XXX	OOO
	XXX	OOO
	XXX	OOO
	XXX	OOO
	XXX	OOO
Clients	XXX	OOO

BETRAYAL BY SPIRIT

In Chicago, fifty-four Catholic priests are banned from their pastoral roles because of sexual misconduct with children. Father Porter, a priest in Minnesota, has had over 240 victims come forward and accuse him of sexual abuse. Still another has had 162 counts of sexual misconduct with children filed against him. In that case, the out-of-court settlements thus far exceed $20 million. A religious order has settled a $3.5 million suit and faces imminent bankruptcy because of others yet to be settled. A treatment center that specializes in work with clergy has come under sharp criticism as being little more than a "warehouse" for the bishops that failed to do serious rehabilitation.

In the midst of all this controversy, a disturbing study of two religious orders for women emerged from Johns Hopkins University. The study documents that over 80 percent of these religious women were sexually abused as children. A new book suggests that only 2 percent of Catholic clergy remain celibate over their careers, and that 6 percent are involved with children. Worse, the author documents that some of the cover-ups involve bishops who have also been involved with children.

The pastoral abuse of children has grabbed the public's attention. Yet other stories are emerging, including revelations about compulsive prostitution, exploitation of pastoral counseling clients, and clergy living double lives of public abstinence and private relationships. As the revelations continue, a deep despair grows; something is very wrong—and has been for a long time.

Protestant and Jewish congregations have also suffered devastating stories of sexual transgressions. The most blatant have been the televangelists whose careers and empires have crumbled because of sexual improprieties. One of the most successful went before his faithful and asked for forgiveness, only to be arrested for prostitution several weeks later. He made the news again when it was discovered that after his arrest he went out that same night and procured another prostitute. Another Protestant minister preached nationwide crusades against pornography, only to be arrested for the production and distribution of child pornography. His followers were stunned. Another well-known minister was arrested for bank robbery. Why had he done it? He had $40,000 in credit card charges for using prostitutes. An Episcopalian bishop committed suicide because his sexual misconduct was about to become public.

One temple was riven apart when word spread that a

beloved and respected rabbi had been sexual with many women in his congregation. Ironically, down the street in the same suburban community, a Lutheran congregation learned that they had been found liable—as a congregation—for the sexual abuse of a teenager by one of their ministers, thus setting a legal precedent.

Media exposure of the problem has been extensive, though it tends to emphasize the sensational over the substantive. The effort of the public to understand has been important in helping underscore the issue of clerical abuse. More serious journalistic efforts in the genre of Burkett and Bruni's *A Gospel of Shame* documented more fully the impact of sexual exploitation.[8] We see in their interviews the pain of the survivors and the congregations. Clinicians have written about the nature of pastoral sexual abuse such as Fortune's *Is Nothing Sacred? When Sex Invades the Pastoral Relationship*[9] or Berry's *Lead Us Not into Temptation: Catholic Priests and the Sexual Abuse of Children*.[10] An ethnographic approach by clinician Richard Sipe in *Sex, Priests, and Power* describes clearly the culture and beliefs within the Catholic Church that foster sexual misconduct.[11] Shupe's sociological investigation of the phenomenon in *In the Name of All That Is Holy* underscores these issues across all denominations.[12]

One conclusion all these reports share is that what little data we have is but part of the metaphorical iceberg. Professionals in general see this in reporting rates. A detailed study of reporting rates suggests that, depending on the category, the actual number of assaults may be from two to twenty times greater than the number of assaults reported by authorities. Studies of offenders also document numbers far in excess of what was expected. An average sex offender commits at least two different types of assaults, and will commit many assaults before being caught. For example, child molesters average 281 assaults against 150 victims. Sex offenders in general report over 520 offenses per person. These figures are for the culture at large. How much more difficult it is to report when our offender is a beloved clergy person.

A few empirical studies of clergy and sexual misconduct do exist. Two general surveys indicate that 10 percent of clergy self-reported sexual contact with congregants.[13, 14] Another indicates 3 percent of Christian therapists have acted on sexual feelings toward clients (Leong).[15] These figures would parallel studies of psychotherapists and psychiatrists, which report results ranging from 5 to 15 percent having had sexual contact with clients.

Even fewer studies exist on the victims of clergy, although it is generally agreed that the impact on survivors of sexual abuse by spiritual leaders is greater than survivors of other forms of power abuse. Since part of coping with trauma is spiritual, sexual abuse by a spiritual leader further complicates the recovery process. Barbara McLaughlin found that as a result of their abuse, victims do not attend church or synagogue and their ability to trust church officials (and God) is impaired or permanently damaged. She suggests further that the victim's relationship with God may cease to grow developmentally because of the abuse. The victim remains frozen spiritually to the time when the abuse occurred.[16]

In order to make sense out of this, we can look at what Viktor Frankl wrote about the Nazi concentration camps. The Nazis had a rule that if you interfered with the suicide of an inmate, you would be shot on the spot. The only way the prisoners could help each other survive was to ask those in despair what gave their life meaning. What Frankl learned in the Holocaust was that those who survived were the ones who could make meaning out of suffering. My experience with survivors of trauma is that every journey or recovery depends on the survivor coming to a point where all that person has gone through means something.

Betrayal by the spirit means that the person who betrays the victim also plays a critical role in the resources the victim has for defining meaning. The victim's spiritual path is blocked. The fundamental question all victims have to answer for themselves is: "Why do bad things happen to good people?" It is a far more troubling question when the cause of the problem is supposed to be the resource for the answer. Whether it be a new cult or a traditional religious denomination, people are searching for meaning. That search and the vulnerability it produces may be used as part of the seduction or the promise. Trauma bonding is exponential under these circumstances because it blocks the critical process of trusting anything meaningful and leaves only the option of despair.

At the Meadows, we often see victims of spiritual abuse. As part of their treatment experience they spend some very moving time in the Sonoran desert, where the program is located. Something about being in an environment so profoundly quiet allows a person finally to hear her inner voice, a voice that had been lost. The person is often so moved that tears shut away for decades suddenly flow. And each time it happens, I am reminded of the human capacity to reach beyond suffering, no matter how ill-deserved the pain.

REFLECTING ON BETRAYAL

The starting point for all trauma survivors is a complete acceptance of the betrayal. Without that window on their reality they will be locked in a circular program—like a computer when it cannot get unstuck. You literally have to reboot the computer to get reality functioning again. Human systems are the same.

This chapter has explored betrayal in all its forms and in stark detail. In the next chapter, I'll focus on our need to understand what makes betrayal bonds so strong.

This chapter ends with a series of activities under the title of "Your History of Seduction." Take the time to read it over in its entirety, then complete it carefully. At this point, you may want to find a journal, tablet or folder in which to keep all your work from this book. Some people have actually done these exercises on their computer and placed them in a special file. As the book progresses and you continue to complete more exercises, you will find it extremely helpful to be able to refer to your earlier work.

Take your time. Do not push yourself. Allow the material to guide. If you get stuck or find it difficult, talk to people who know you and support you. Be gentle with yourself. Take breaks, but do not skip the work.

YOUR HISTORY OF SEDUCTION

Reflect on your life and select at least five people (ten if you can) who have exploited you using seduction. Do not restrict yourself to sexual issues, but expand your list to include all forms of exploitation. Write the names of each person. Record after each individual the promise made (story, fantasy, dream, omission). After the promise, write the real intent or agenda you now know was true. An example is provided. You can do this in your book or you may wish to use your journal, a computer or a special tablet. We will be using this information later.

Example:

Gene A.   Pledged that if I met   After three years, I
                 my performance   exceeded all my goals,
                 criteria, I would be   he picked a fight and
                 made partner. When   fired me. He never
                 I did, he added that   intended to bring me
                 I had to do it for   into the business.
                 three years.

Individual:	Promise made:	True agenda or intent:
1.		
2.		
3.		
4.		
5.		
6.		
7.		
8.		
9.		
10.		

Analyzing your list

The following activities will deepen your understanding of the work you have done. Record your answers in a journal, computer file or dedicated tablet. They will be very important for your later work in this book and for your recovery. The temptation will be to say, "I have the idea" and move on to the next section. Doing this thoroughly—even if painstaking—will substantially lay the foundation for what you now need to do.

1. Place a *T* under the name of each individual who used terror or fear to manipulate you. Place a *P* under the name of each individual who abused his power over you such as an employer, therapist, teacher or parent. Place an *I* under the name of each individual who exploited the intimacy of your relationship, such as a friend, spouse, family member or therapist. Place an *S* under the

name of each individual who exploited your values or sources of meaning (spirit) in your life.

2. After you have put the letters under their names, notice if you have any patterns. Are there specific letters that appear over and over again? For example, do you have a lot of *T*s and *P*s? Record in your paperwork what you think this means. Where does this pattern come from?

3. Some individuals on your list may be seducing you in many ways. Perhaps it was even difficult to select which seduction to record. For each individual, make a separate list of all the seductions and what the true intent was for each.

4. Notice if there are any commonalities across the promises made. Is there any common story or promise to which you are susceptible? What is it about that scenario that makes you so vulnerable? What hope or need kept you going?

5. What efforts to stop did you make? What happened to those efforts? In what ways could you have taken care of yourself better?

6. What do the various people on your list have in common? Notice if there are any personality traits, habits or qualities they share. Does a type emerge? If so, who in your family or early childhood history is similar? Write a description of the "typical" person who can seduce you. What sense do you make of how that came to be?

4

WHAT MAKES TRAUMA BONDS STRONGER?

Today, our society is caught in the grip of superficial values—glamour, glitter, materialism, a pathological emphasis on youth, a neglect of the elderly, the handicapped. Families are being broken up under the impact of a frenzied desire for success. Violence is glorified and paraded in front of children every day on the media.

Basic human value, basic decency, kindness, cooperation are less and less evident. Economic pressures and psychological pressures mount. More and more individuals feel unhappiness—and helplessness—in their acquisitiveness for pleasure and accumulation in this selfish society. They turn to artificial stimulants, they lose touch with themselves. Their problems, their insecurities mount, and become despondency. The suicides of society cause us to reflect on the terrible trend.

REVEREND JAMES JONES
ANTI-SUICIDAL SPEECH IN 1977 DELIVERED FROM THE GOLDEN GATE
BRIDGE EIGHTEEN MONTHS BEFORE THE JONESTOWN DEATHS

The new venture was so exciting. Jan, Phil and Don were forming a new company based on breakthrough research Phil had done as a biochemist. The idea was to start the company by marketing products based on Phil's work, then build the company by developing other biotechnology products. They would have fun, run their own show and end up wealthy. Jan and Don were experienced executives at another biomedical firm. Don had been president and CEO, and Jan had been head of product development. Every meeting they had together was filled with laughter and excitement.

They started with Phil signing a licensing agreement that gave the company the right to manufacture and sell the products he developed. That way the company could get started. The partnership agreements were much more complex and not so urgent, since everyone agreed in principle as to what was to happen. What followed was a rush of frenzied activity to get the product to market so that the company could get a cash flow going. Everybody was working so hard that the partnership agreement kept being postponed because of financial pressure.

But some things bothered Phil. It started when he visited Don's former company to discuss a matter unrelated to the new business. The company had been sold as part of an acquisition, which was why Don had left. The remaining employees described their relief at the end of Don's "reign of terror." Anybody who even saw Don reported the "Don sighting." Everyone took turns on the "Don watch" so that nobody would have to run into him. Phil wrote this off to Don having presided over a substantial and unpopular downsizing. In fact, it was a comfort to know Don could make the hard decisions. Still, their comments bothered him.

Another thing that bothered Phil was that shortly after they started production, Jan and Don sat down with him and let him know they were now living together. They were to be married because Jan was pregnant. They wanted to assure Phil that this would not slow down the startup; they just wanted to be up front with him before they signed the partnership papers. Phil was very congratulatory but also very disturbed. Should there ever be a dispute, he would lose.

Other disturbing things started happening. A critical vendor who had worked many years with Phil had done a credit check on Don. The vendor told Phil he would not process orders he had received because Don was on the verge of bankruptcy. Phil gave the vendor assurance that the bills would be paid.

When told of the vendor's response, Don criticized him, then got upset with Phil for selecting the vendor. Other vendors started calling Phil and reporting that Don was losing his temper over really small issues. Jan reassured Phil that it was simply stress and that she would help Don keep cool. Then one vendor became so outraged with Don's tirades that the president of that company gave orders that no one could do business with Phil and his partners. Jan again assured Phil there would be no problem.

Phil finally acknowledged he was in trouble when his bankers called and asked to have lunch. They reported to Phil that Jan and Don had been in to see them about a credit line for the company. In the course of the meetings about the credit line three things became clear. First, they asked to use Phil's assets for the credit line since they had none. Second, they revealed that they would be the principal owners of the company. No plans existed for Phil to be a partner. And finally, they talked disparagingly about Phil. They said his technology was excellent but that they did not want to work with him long-term.

The bankers revealed that by giving Phil this information they were violating Federal regulations about client confidentiality. However, they had known Phil to be a good customer for many years. Phil had also told them how excited he was about the new partnership. The bankers wanted Phil to know that he was about to be swindled out of his hard-won research.

They saw his potential partners as dangerous and advised him to sever his relationship with them. Within a day of the lunch, several vendors called to indicate either nonpayment or a serious diversion of funds. His partners were now guilty of fraud. Jan and Don went bankrupt. There were suits, counter-suits and losses to go around.

This story is about much more than a business failure. Some further data creates a much more complex picture. Phil was an incest and sexual abuse victim. The fact that he ignored or dis-counted warnings that he was being exploited was actually a life pattern, and resulted in a lot of hard work and creativity that were all for naught.

Don was a physical abuse victim. He had a significant weight problem because of compulsive overeating, and a compulsive debting problem. But it was his raging that had cost him both marriages and businesses. Jan was a battered wife who could not end the relationship with her violent husband until she started the affair with her boss, Don. Jan was also an alcoholic who dismissed her sponsor and recovery friends when they raised questions about Don. Put these facts together and it's not hard to understand why the business failed.

There is deception and exploitation in this scenario. Don is sexually involved with a married employee. Don and Jan love bomb Phil so that he will hand over his technology and over-look their relationship and the absence of partnership papers. The bankers violate legal statutes and deceive Don and Jan in order to help Phil. And there is rescuing. Phil saves the deal by intervening with vendors. Jan intervenes on behalf of Don with Phil over Don's temper tantrums. The bankers work to rescue Phil from being fraudulently deceived. Jan's friends work to rescue Jan from Don. The irony is that Don and Jan had initially presented themselves as rescuers who would save Phil from the big corporations that would take advantage of him. They promised he would be an owner.

Lurking in the background of this scenario is a very large,

heavyset man whose rage is legendary. In fact, Phil was to learn that people had a hard time getting over Don. The president of the company that did the leveraged buyout of Don's previous company told Phil years later that he still had unresolved anger relative to the way that Don had handled the merger. Former employees told Phil that it was a long time before they stopped their "Don watches." Years later, vendors would shake their heads about the whole episode. Terror and intimidation were Don's stock in trade. But for him it was simply the coping skill he had learned to deal with the abuse in his family.

You might say, "What a soap opera!" Exactly. Soap operas are intentionally built on betrayal, deception, exploitation and terror. The intensity created from these ingredients is addictive. That's why there are so many loyal viewers. It is in these soap opera environments that betrayal bonds thrive. They are never simple. Convoluted plots always enliven the script. If it were simple, it would be to easy to detach. Phil, Don and Jan couldn't detach because they were hooked on the drama of it all. Business and personal life dysfunctions overlap. Betrayal, addiction and trauma weave a design of continually recycled wounds that create an overarching pattern of compulsive relationships. Whether corporate or familial, the same abuse patterns appear.

While these patterns are not simple, it is possible to discern what makes them so strong. If we break down the patterns into specific component parts, they become clear and then no longer hold any power.

There are eleven ways that betrayal bonds are made stronger. They are:

1. when there are repetitive cycles of abuse
2. when the victim and the victimizer believe in their own uniqueness
3. when high intensity is mistaken for intimacy
4. when there is confusion about love

5. when there are increasing amounts of fear
6. when children are faced with terror
7. when there is a history of abuse
8. when exploitation endures over time
9. when the community, family or social structure reacts in the extremes
10. when there is a familiar role and script to be fulfilled
11. when victims and victimizers switch roles of rescue and abuse

Each of these conditions adds to the emotional bond and deepens addictive attachment.

WHEN THERE ARE REPETITIVE CYCLES OF ABUSE

In domestic abuse there is a predictable cycle. First there is a buildup stage. It combines both intensity and fear. As the tension rises, family members obsess about the outcome. Although it is probably inevitable, there is always the hope that compliant action (the proverbial walking on eggshells) will postpone the perpetrator's rage. For the sake of example, let us say that this stage lasts four weeks. Then the outbreak of violence occurs, that violence may last only ninety seconds. From my counseling experience, I can tell you that a great deal of damage can be done in ninety seconds.

The violence is immediately followed by what is called the "honeymoon" stage. The perpetrator experiences the relief of tension and then is filled with shame over what he has done. He apologizes with deep remorse and pledges with all the sincerity he can muster that he will never do it again. Further, he demonstrates his change of heart by starting a new courtship. He showers her with gifts and devotion. He says the things she has always wanted to hear from him. He is tender in the most endearing, lovable ways. He's Lucy Van Pelt promising Charlie

Brown that this time she will hold the football. Let us say this period also lasts four weeks. This is the time of promise—it is the story, the dream.

In part this is an intimacy disorder, for as soon as she starts to recommit to the relationship, he starts distancing himself. The intensity begins to build again. He feels trapped or jealous or possessive or something else that distances him from her. Imagine that a relationship is a circle. For true intimacy to take place, both must stay in the circle at the same time. In abusive relationships with this type of cyclical nature, neither person can allow him- or herself to stay. She must leave the circle when he is abusive. He can only be abusive when he has left the circle. When the "love bomb" works, she is brought back into the mini-cult of their relationship. The terror and fear begin to intensify.

Notice that throughout this eight-week scenario, there is always something intense and absorbing. In the buildup phase you have the incredible intensity, high risk and obsession we identified earlier as traumatic arousal. We know that people do become "hooked" on high risk, especially if it involves sex, romance or power. The actual violence is not the goal here. It serves to give credibility to the terror and to signal the shift back to the honeymoon stage. Nor is the romance of the honeymoon stage just about reconciliation. It is also the soothing, medicating and nurturing that are part of betrayal bonding. Both partners are obsessed with whether she is going to accept the promise again. Neither partner has to come to grips with the pain or patterns of their lives. No one can begin to understand the drama of O. J. and Nicole Simpson, or any other couple caught in the domestic abuse cycle, without knowing how that cycle engages its participants.

Traditional patterns of addiction are also present within this cycle. The abuse of drugs, alcohol, sex and food are common-place for the participants. Nearly 75 percent of all wives of alcoholics, for example, have been threatened, and 45 percent have been assaulted by their addicted partners. Alcohol and drugs may be used to rationalize violent behavior. Family members and perpetrators will blame their behavior on drug and alcohol abuse.[1] Not true. It is simply one layer of compulsion on top of another, layers that defined and managed betrayal cycles going back for decades, even generations.

Sexual addiction is also part of the drama. Compulsive sexual violence can emerge in many forms:

> pressure to use alcohol and drugs before sex
>
> insistence on the use of sexual performance enhancers
>
> derogatory comments during sex
>
> forced involvement in unsafe sex or group sex
>
> forced risk for unwanted pregnancy
>
> requirement to undergo cosmetic surgery
>
> humiliating, degrading practices
>
> some types of dress and role play
>
> public sex (exhibitionism, voyeurism, swapping)
>
> use of bondage
>
> rape or sexual assault

Similarly, compulsive food use can be something the abuser cannot control and obesity can be a way to deflect unwanted attention. What follows is a summary of domestic abuse characteristics that underscore the involvement of addictions and the repetitive, compulsive nature of the cycles themselves.

> Men who assault female partners are more likely to have witnessed or experienced violence in childhood, abuse alcohol, be sexually assaultive and be at risk for perpetration of violence against children. In fact, 63 percent of abusers report having seen their mothers abused.

On average, in Canada, a woman will be assaulted 3.5 times before contacting the police. In fact, among battered women who are first identified in a medical setting, 75 percent will go on to suffer repeated abuse.

Many women who make repeated attempts to get help are told the violence must be their own fault, and in some cases find that revealing the truth of what happened makes people so uncomfortable that disclosure negatively affects their treatment.

About 50 percent of abusers have a problem with alcohol and 33 percent with illicit drugs.

Nearly 25 percent of women in the United States will be abused by a current or former partner sometime during their lives.

47 percent of husbands who beat their wives do so three or more times a year.

30 percent of women murdered were killed by their husbands or boyfriends, and it is estimated that 53 percent of female murder victims were killed by a current or former partner.

In 45 to 59 percent of child abuse cases, the mother is also being abused.

Of women over the age of 30 who have been raped, 58 percent were raped in the context of an abusive relationship.

Notice as well that the engaging elements of the domestic abuse cycle have parallels in other forms of exploitation. Incest also has cycles of abuse, with predictable stages of arousal and relief for both abuser and child. Child researchers De Young and Lowry describe in detail the typical cycle of the incest family. In describing the scenario from the father's perspective, they write: "This pattern of buildup, the act of abuse and relief can become habituated, and the parent's growing dependency on the child for both arousal and relief can preclude his ever seeking other, more appropriate, sexual partners. Traumatic bonding to the child has taken place."[2]

In corporate abuse, the employees who wait for another wave of terror know this cycle. In the case of Don, Jan, Phil and the failed partnership with which we started this chapter, they each played their parts in the cycle very well. They learned the roles in their respective families and played out the scene in a different arena. If it repeats so that it is a predictable cycle, it adds to the trauma bond.

WHEN THE VICTIM AND THE VICTIMIZER BELIEVE IN THEIR OWN UNIQUENESS

She has been seeing her analyst three times a week for nine years. She has been having sex with him during those sessions for seven years. And she pays for the sessions in which they have sex. On Fridays she comes to his office and types for him. She doesn't know why his wife refuses to meet his needs because he is such a good man. He has been so helpful to so many people and so helpful to her; she cannot be grateful enough. Sometimes she actually enjoys sex with him. But mostly she is content with knowing how special their relationship is. She sees the other women patients in his waiting room, and the attractive nurse. They are absolutely gorgeous. And out of all these women, he has selected her to meet his special needs. She knows he would not do it with anyone else, and she gets so much extra help because of their special relationship.

As long as she is convinced of her uniqueness in his life, the secret is safe. When she finds out she is only one of eighty, she is enraged. But until that point the "promise" works. She believes she is the only one.

The relationship is also secret, which means no one can raise any issues about it. This covenant of betrayal can be found in incest families (Dad picked me out of all the kids), in sexual misconduct by clergy (he picked me out of the whole congregation), or in schools (I was picked out of all of the students). The victim does not see the sexual exploitation as betrayal. The real betrayal is if the secret gets out and Dad goes to jail, Father can no longer be a priest or the teacher can no longer teach. In the covenant of betrayal the victim accepts the story and the promise, which justifies the feeling of uniqueness. Telling the secret would betray the dream and the meaning it carries. It is like the science fiction thriller in which an alien has been planted inside the victim. Life can go on if it is not disturbed. But it will destroy its host if awakened.

More than likely the victimizer will believe the story as well. Jerry was a psychiatrist who specialized in family therapy. His abilities were truly extraordinary. He was recognized nationally and internationally because of his ability to articulate family dynamics so quickly and clearly. Patients flocked from all over the world. Therapists filled his seminars to see if they could perform the same kind of magic he did. Unfortunately, Jerry saw himself as unique as well. He believed that he was above the conventions and rules that other therapists had to observe. Jerry was convinced that he was able to take certain liberties with his patients in order to accelerate their progress. If women could learn about how to be sexual with him, he could use his insight and personality to help the patient make a shift in her sexual well-being.

Over one hundred women came forward to testify to Jerry's sexual conduct in the office. As a result, the state board of medical examiners took his license away. For months it was front-page news. Yet amazingly, patients still flocked to see him. It was as if nothing had happened—except that now people paid cash because their health insurance would no longer cover their visits. The patients who now saw him believed that the medical establishment could not tolerate his ability to challenge traditional medical concepts. Jerry, too, believed in his own uniqueness.

When uniqueness means that you are not like other people and do not have human limitations, you enter the arena that the Greek playwrights called *tragedy*. Greek heroes often had the same tragic flaws: *hubris,* or excessive pride. They had set themselves above other human beings. To the Greeks that meant to make yourself unto a god. That was always a mistake. Greek gods were not very tolerant of mortals who looked for godhood. Oedipus, Sisyphus, Tantalus and Jason all suffered because of their excessive pride and their refusal to accept their own limits. Their myths describe otherwise noble, likable, attractive people who suffered horrible fates because of their tragic flaw of hubris. It's the same with people who victimize. They can be wonderfully gifted and even do many wonderful things. That, in fact, makes the "promise" even more believable. Yet when they fail to accept human limitation, and when they believe they are not subject to the same constraints as others, they enter the arena of tragedy.

Here are some ways such entitlement can develop:

> Some people were so damaged while growing up that they came to trust no one and to regard all rules, laws and limits as applying to others and not themselves. They are often angry and well-disguised. Clinicians define these people as *sociopaths* or *antisocial* individuals.

> Some people had parents who were so obsessed with them that they met all their adult needs by focusing on their child. These children, in turn, became so obsessed with themselves that they do not realize they are having an impact on others. Clinicians term these people *narcissists.*

> Some people were so abused that they manage their anxiety with compulsive use of alcohol, drugs, sex, food or gambling. Their obsession and preoccupation

so distort reality that they rationalize their entitled behavior. Clinicians call them addicts.

Some people grew up in families of extraordinary wealth, power and fame, which insulated them from accountability and a healthy sense of human limitation. As adults, they often feel very trepidatious about the loss of their status. At the same time, they feel that the public invades their privacy and that their heritage entitles them to do whatever is necessary to meet their needs and preserve their image.

Some people, because of great talent and hard work, rise to positions of great power, such as physicians, members of the clergy or attorneys. They may see themselves as having worked harder, achieved more, sacrificed more, and been smarter and tougher than others. Therefore, they believe that they are more deserving.

The paths to entitlement are myriad. In a recent study of sexual misconduct by members of the clergy, for example, researchers found that over 55 percent were alcoholics or drug addicts or both, 50 percent were sex addicts, and 33 percent were compulsive. The compulsive disorders included eating, spending, working and a variety of high-risk activities. There were also identifiable personality disorders, including a large number of diagnosable narcissists, but also clergymen who were extremely dependent, obsessive-compulsive and histrionic (highly dramatic).[3] Not surprising was that they also came from intrusive, abusive families.

Organizations and movements also have their sense of entitlement. Jonestown, the Holocaust, the Japanese followers of those who put poisonous gas in the subways—all shared a sense of uniqueness. Group hubris simply has the effect of making tragedy exponential.

The point is this: Both victim and victimizer draw energy for their traumatic bonding from a sense of uniqueness. In fact, part of the covenant between them, if it were written down, would start: "Because we are unique . . . "

WHEN HIGH INTENSITY IS MISTAKEN FOR INTIMACY

When you come from a family in which members showed little emotion or affection, and you meet someone around whom there are lots of feelings, you might perceive this as intimacy. At least there are feelings. But if the feelings are about high drama, betrayal and passionate reconciliations, it is not intimacy. It is intensity. And it is both adsorbing and addictive.

The addiction is about high arousal and high risk. In the mid-1970s addiction specialists were already noticing that people could become compulsive about high-risk situations. Solomon at Brown University described sky divers and race car drivers who would continually put themselves at risk when it was clearly insane to do so.[4] McClelland at Harvard also researched CEOs of large corporations who could not leave their offices because they were so addicted to the high drama of acquisitions and buyouts.[5] In fact, the character Sherman McCoy in the novel *Bonfire of the Vanities,* by Tom Wolfe, epitomizes this type of executive, the one who sacrifices all for living on the edge.[6] This character is famous for his soliloquy on being a "Master of the Universe" capable of living in high-risk situations. McCoy is a character written in the Greek tradition of hubris. In many ways this type of arousal is similar to the risk of compulsive gambling. In relationships, the biggest gamble of all is the high-risk relationship.

Intensity exists in relationships when there are betrayal and victim/victimizer scenarios. Intensity thrives on fear and arousal—especially sexual arousal or the fear of sexual betrayal. Return to our circle of intimacy analogy where to be intimate, both have to be in the circle at the same time. Intense relationships often have one in and one out of the circle. There is always the prospect of more betrayal and abandonment. High drama becomes a way to manage anxiety. Dramatic exits, for example, act out the anxiety, rather than use the tension for healthy problem solving. Conflict, in fact, is more likely to be resolved through escalation than resolution. Episode follows episode as the cycles repeat.

Intimacy, in contrast, starts with mutuality and respect. There is neither exploitation by abuse of power, nor betrayal of trust. Passion flows from vulnerability and care—and is a function of the soul. Intimacy relies on safety and patience. Healthy intimacy usually has no secrets. Intensity requires secrecy and develops from it. Intimacy pushes partners to grow. Intensity serves as a distraction from oneself and limits the possibility of growth. Conflicts that arise in intimacy result in negotiation and a clear understanding about fair fighting. Absent are the fear and anxiety of intensity. Constancy and vulnerability create more of the epic than the episodic. Figure 4.1 summarizes the differences between intensity and intimacy.

Trauma bonds thrive on intensity. I had a woman client describe intensity in reference to her experiences with traumatic bonding. She said, "Intensity is like Styrofoam. It takes up space but has no substance."

WHEN THERE ARE INCREASING AMOUNTS OF FEAR

In almost all beginning psychology courses there is a section describing an amazing phenomenon: People are more sexually attractive to us when we associate them with danger. Psychology professors describe experiments in which they show students pictures of young people in a neutral context and then show pictures of the same people on a swaying

Figure 4.1. Intensity vs. Intimacy

DIMENSION	INTENSITY	INTIMACY
Roles:	victim/victimizer	mutual, respectful
Feelings:	fear and arousal	passion and vulnerability
Commitment:	one in/one out	involved and enduring
Prospects:	threats of betrayal/ abandonment	safety and patience
Anxiety:	high drama	problem resolution
Problems:	no structure/rules	fair fight contract
Development:	high distraction	high growth
Openness:	built on secrecy	no secrets
Conflict:	escalation	negotiation
Scenario:	episode begets episode	constancy

bridge. Somehow, these same people are more sexually attractive when on a perilous, swinging bridge than when in a safe, neutral setting.

Actually, it is more complex than romantic interest that fear simply escalates. Countless investigations show that fear intensifies all human attachment. In fact, all forms of vertebrate species studied, including birds, dogs, primates and humans, appear to have this trait. Fear deepens bonding. Traumatic violence in relationships (especially if positive episodes moderate even occasionally, as in cycles) greatly increases the intensity of the attachment bond.

A series of neurobiological changes occurs in the body during intense fear. In adults and especially in children, the actual biological strata of the brain can be altered. This results in the reactivity and other trauma options described in chapter 1. The parts of the brain designed to protect yourself gain dominance and may override other parts of the brain that limit reactive responses. A growing body of evidence indicates a neurochemical "scarring" can occur throughout the body. This means that severe trauma can leave a mark that can be discerned in every system of the body. That is how pervasive the impact of terror can be.[7]

Fear escalates the reactivity of the body, which in turn escalates all the survival options: arousal, blocking, splitting, abstinence, shame, repetition and bonding. Consider the story of Jonestown and the willing deaths of over 900 people. They were a mixture of senior citizens, whites, blacks, hippies, doctors, middle-class executives, orphans and disadvantaged youths whom Jones personally had adopted. They were members of the People's Temple, who had left America to set up a better society in the jungle of Guyana. What they created was a nightmare of terror. Jonestown was more like a concentration camp. Jones controlled all property and income, he worked to weaken family ties, he created a caste system to control what people said, he controlled any possibility of escape, and he worked to control thoughts and emotions. There were beatings. He sexually exploited his members. As one investigator described Jones at the end:

His paranoia was severe; his megalomania pervasive, insisting all members address him as "Father," and he seemed to be progressively falling victim to disease, a lust for money, power, guns, sex, and drugs. His leadership toward the end was punitive, narcissistic and paranoid to the extreme.[8]

Congressman Leo Ryan had heard of the plight of some members of the Jonestown community and flew down to secure the freedom of people who wished to leave the community. During the confrontation that ensued, some of the members did want to leave. As they went to board the plane they were shot, along with Ryan and his aides. Reverend Jones then asked for the supreme sacrifice of his followers to show their disappointment in the American system. Nine hundred thirteen people followed him to their deaths. They were victims of violence, sadism, sexual exploitation and murder—yet they followed.

Some might say this is an isolated event. Not so. History is filled with such examples. Here is another: Synanon was established as a therapeutic community to deal with drug addiction in 1958. Over the years it became a closed system and evolved into a religious cult. It ended with the founder, Charles Dederich, being arrested for conspiracy to commit murder. Ironically, he was extremely intoxicated at the time of his arrest. William Whyte describes part of that evolution:

> As Synanon moved closer to the status of a cult, Dederich introduced a series of conformity tests that would drive out all but the most committed Synanon members. These tests included mandatory shaving of heads of all members, mandatory vasectomies and abortions and, in late 1977, Synanon couples were required to "change partners." . . . What is amazing in this story is not Dederich's demand to change partners, but the fact that over 700 Synanon members complied with this request.[9]

Control makes the fear. The fear deepens the bond.

WHEN CHILDREN ARE FACED WITH TERROR

Trauma bonding for children appears to be more severe. First, they are experiencing their primary attachments. If they experience terror in those relationships, the mind creates deep patterns and scripts. Relationships with primary caregivers create a relationship template that will be used across a lifetime. Further, children who experience traumatic bonding often exhibit the following characteristics:

> They have an all or nothing response to emotional stimulation.

> They compulsively seek out similar situations to reexpose themselves to similar types of people.

> They experience significant biochemical changes in norepinephrine, dopamine, serotonin and endogenous opioids because of stress depletion, and their needs now exceed their ability to produce.

> They respond to further stressors in hyperreactive fashion.

> They need caregivers to help modulate their reactivity, but the caregivers instead create more trauma.

> They may only remember their emotional reactions and not the actual events because of the insufficient maturation of brain function.

The implications are threefold. First, children have a hard time understanding their own reactions. This in turn creates shame and more anxiety. Second, they have what traumatologists call *addiction to the trauma*.[10] They deliberately seek or re-create the abuse experience. Finally, their initial trauma bond is more intense because of their vulnerability, which makes subsequent relationships of a similar nature more probable. They have difficulty internalizing either moderation or self-protective boundaries.

WHEN THERE ALSO IS A HISTORY OF ABUSE

Let us say there are two current victims of sexual harassment. One is a victim of prior abuse going back to childhood. The other has a history of normal childhood and adult development. Both will suffer symptoms of post-traumatic stress. Both are vulnerable to traumatic bonding. The one with the abuse history, however, will have more severe reactions to stress and an increased potential for traumatic bonding.

The problem is admitting it. With abuse comes loyalty to the abuser. With loyalty come secrecy and denial. The abuser threatens that if there is any disclosure, the result will be tragedy—exile from the family, destruction of the family, severe punishment or death of the victim, or any ultimate threat. Whether the threat is real or simply used to control the victim, it becomes part of the interior world of the victim. The victim starts to take on the views of the perpetrator and uphold the perpetrator's position in the family or organization. William Tollefson describes this loyalty:

> *Sexual abuse victims do not view the breaking of the trust bond by the abuser as a betrayal. But if the victim ever discloses the secret, it is then that the ultimate betrayal has occurred, and that can not be forgiven. If the abuser is not around, the victim will carry out the sentence in any form—from addictive behavior to self abusive behavior.*[11]

As a therapist, I cannot count the times a breakthrough has occurred when the patient faces the question: Who in the family would benefit by your life being such a mess? Oftentimes it is the abuser. The victim, who leads a life filled with relationship failures, addiction, career catastrophes, arrests and high drama, has no credibility, has taken all focus off the abuser, and has used personal chaos to deflect questions of accountability.

Sometimes it helps simply to review categories of abuse to see if they fit your experiences. I have provided the following Abuse Inventory upon which you can reflect. Completing it will provide you with information that will help you as you proceed with this book. Notice if you feel as though you are breaking rules by completing it. You may wish to write about it in the notes you are keeping.

ABUSE INVENTORY

Betrayal bonds are more intense when there is history of abuse. Sometimes looking at the categories of abuse can help you broaden your own self-awareness. The following checklist and worksheet will help you assess the extent of your abuse during your childhood. To cope with your own abuse, you may have minimized the impact the abuse had on your life. Now is the time to recognize the abuse for what it was. Know that it was not your fault, and recognize your powerlessness over it.

Read over each of the three categories of abuse (emotional, physical and sexual). Fill in the information in the spaces next to the items that apply to you. For each type of abuse, record the information to the best of your memory.

These may be powerful memories. You may wish to use your journal pages to record details and memories. You may also wish to consult with your therapist, friends or support group.

In chapter 1, we learned that to view trauma, we must look at two factors. First, how significant the impact was; second, how often the abuse happened. So, for example, you could have something happen just a few times, but it may have had a very harmful effect on you. Similarly, something done may not be in itself that harmful, but it may cause severe stress simply because it happens repeatedly. Look at the above figure to see the relationship between frequency and impact of abuse.

For example, if you experienced touch deprivation occasionally, you may not consider the deprivation very important. However, if you were deprived constantly, you may view your situation quite differently. It is not just the quantity that is important, but how you experienced the abuse.

Figure 4.2. Abuse Inventory

Age How old were you when the abuse started?

Abusing Who abused you? Father, stepfather, mother, stepmother, adult
persons relative, adult friend, adult neighbor, neighborhood children,
professional person, brother or sister, stranger?

Frequency How often did it happen? Daily, two to three times a week,
weekly, monthly? You may use the following scale: 1=one
time; 2=seldom; 3=periodically; 4=often; and 5=very often.

FORM OF ABUSE	AGE	FREQUENCY	ABUSING PERSON
Emotional Abuse			
Example: Neglect	3	5	grandparent, father
Neglect (i.e., significant persons are emotionally unavailable; emotional or physical care is inadequate)			
Harassment or malicious tricks			
Being screamed at or shouted at			
Unfair punishments			
Cruel or degrading tasks			
Cruel confinement (e.g., being locked in closet; excessive grounding for long periods)			
Abandonment (e.g., lack of supervision, lack of security, being left or deserted, death or divorce removing primary caregivers)			

FORM OF ABUSE	AGE	FREQUENCY	ABUSING PERSON
Touch deprivation			
No privacy			
Having to hide injuries or wounds from others			
Forced to keep secrets			
Having to take on adult responsibilities as a child			
Having to watch beating of other family members			
Being caught in the middle of parents' fights			
Being blamed for family problems			
Other forms of emotional abuse			
Physical Abuse			
Example: Shoving	8, 18–30	5	Mother, stepfather, spouse
Shoving			
Slapping or hitting			
Scratches or bruises			
Burns			
Cuts or wounds			

FORM OF ABUSE	AGE	FREQUENCY	ABUSING PERSON
Broken bones or fractures			
Damage to internal organs			
Permanent injury			
Beatings or whippings			
Inadequate medical attention			
Pulling and grabbing of hair, ears, etc.			
Sexual Abuse			
Example: Flirtatious and suggestive language	6, 12–17	4	Stranger, adult neighbor
Propositioning			
Inappropriate holding, kissing			
Sexual fondling			
Masturbation			
Oral sex			
Forced sexual activity			
Household voyeurism (inappropriate household nudity, etc.)			
Sexual hugs			
Jokes about your body			

FORM OF ABUSE	AGE	FREQUENCY	ABUSING PERSON
Use of sexualizing language			
Penetration with objects			
Bestiality (forced sex with animals)			
Criticism of your physical or sexual development			
Another's preoccupation with your sexual development			
Other forms of sexual abuse			

For many of us, denying the pain and reality of the abuse that we endured has been a source of our insanity. Accepting our powerlessness is not saying that it was okay; it is recognizing, maybe for the first time, that the abuse was not okay. Until we can accept the fear, anger and sadness, we cannot grieve. It is our grieving that helps us accept our powerlessness.

How has the abuse you received as a child affected you? How do you feel when you reflect on these events? How has abuse impacted your behavior?

WHEN IT INVOLVES TRUSTED FAMILY MEMBERS OR TRUSTED FAMILY FRIENDS AND IT LASTS A LONG TIME

The husband shot his wife as she attempted to leave their driveway in her car. When their oldest son valiantly tried to stop the shooting, the father assaulted him. Newspaper reports about this Oregon family described how the fifty-six-year-old man had murdered his wife who was thirty-six years old. The husband fled into the woods in the midst of one of the worst blizzards to hit northern Oregon. Embedded in the news reports was the fact that this man's wife was also his stepdaughter. They had three children together, including the oldest son whom the father had assaulted. What the news-papers could not prove, but what everyone in town knew, was that his wife was not his stepdaughter. Actually, he had married his real daughter after the mysterious death of his original wife, her mother.

While extreme, this story illustrates the worst that can happen to a victim. There is a growing body of evidence that shows the most distress occurs in victims whose family members or family friends have betrayed them. There is further evidence that part of the problem is that these situations can last for many years, which simply deepens the traumatic bond-ing. Clinicians measure assaults not by the number of events but by over how long a period of time they took place. The variable that emerges from this research is that the impact of trauma is greatest not when strangers commit it but when someone who is known and trusted commits it. So to marry that abuser and thereby make permanent an exploitive relationship would be the worst nightmare possible.

To provide perspective, in the earlier section of this chapter there is a summary of data on domestic abuse. Note the stag-gering percentages of women who are murdered by someone that they know. In the case of the Oregon family, it is clear that there was a betrayal of power and intimacy that resulted in deadly intensity.

Review the Abuse Inventory you just completed. In the sections you completed on the abuser(s), mark the ones who would fit the category of "known and trusted." Record any reflections you have in your notes.

WHEN THE COMMUNITY, FAMILY OR SOCIAL STRUCTURE REACTS IN THE EXTREME

When denominations of various religious traditions had to confront sexual misconduct by their own clergy, one of the options often used was to bury the problem. They simply transferred the clergyman and threw a cloak of secrecy over the issue. No one cajoled the victim to avoid her making a scene or bought her off in any way. They simply denied the reality of the experience in the worst cases. Those in authority feared that the church, and all the good deeds accomplished in its name would lose credibility. As a result of this fear, the church leaders colluded with the perpetrator. The net effect is that traumatic bonding, in the form of secrecy, persisted inside a supportive environment. These leaders committed betrayal by spirit.

This collusion often becomes quite extreme. In the famous Father Porter case, over 240 victims came forward. Instead of facing the issue, the church transferred Porter from one parish to another or from one state to another. To give you an example of how difficult it is to stop this extreme response, one Protestant denomination, after a series of painful situations, developed an abuse policy that outlined what should happen if someone reported sexual misconduct. A task force composed of leaders, victims, their attorneys, therapists and perpetrators carefully thought through the process so it would be fair and helpful to everyone. Shortly after leaders approved it as the official policy, one of the best preachers in the denomination, known for his ability to raise funds, had a report of sexual misconduct filed against him. Church leaders handled it in a secretive way, basically discounting the victim. They handled it this way because of "special" and "unique" circumstances. They ignored the policy because of the power and visibility of the clergyman involved. It was business as usual.

That leaves the victim with one alternative: to go to court. But most victims do not wish to use the legal system. What they want is have people hear them, to see things change, and to have resolution. Victims' advocates say that without significant court settlements, these large systems probably would not have changed their policies of denial and secrecy. The unfortunate result is that the victims place themselves in the adversarial legal system—which adds even more stress. In that arena, the goal is not resolution, but winning. Legal action often has the effect of intensifying betrayal bonds.

WHEN THERE ARE FAMILIAR ROLES OR SCRIPTS

Whenever we see Lucy with the football looking for Charlie Brown, we tend to smile, since we know we are going to revisit the old scenario. Lucy will have some good reason to entice Charlie Brown into taking another run at it. Charlie Brown will resist but will succumb to some new promise. Lucy will pull the ball away and Charlie Brown will be flat on his back again. Lucy will then make some pronouncement that negates her promise. We have seen this script before. We smile because of Lucy's inventiveness and because Charlie Brown's susceptibility reminds us of our own.

It's from our families that we learn to have these Lucy/Charlie Brown relationships. Consider the case of Ken. When I met Ken he was struggling with both depression and drug addiction. As a young adolescent, a man who was a close friend of his parents sexually victimized him. This man was like an "uncle." His parents reacted much like the churches described earlier. They did not believe Ken and punished him severely for making the accusation. So it was for him in his family. Anytime he said something uncomfortable to the rest of the family, they scapegoated him. An example of this took place when he was in his early thirties and his wife related to his mother something Ken had said. Ken's mother, a raging alcoholic, ordered his brothers to beat him up, which they did. As

PEANUTS reprinted by permission of United Feature Syndicate, Inc.

a result of the beating, he was admitted to the emergency room with severe head trauma. These dramatic confrontations filled the family history. At one point one of his brothers attempted to drown him. When asked why he did not leave, Ken answered that this was his family. It was easier to medicate his pain by using drugs. The truth just brought him pain. Leaving would risk even more punishment.

Ken had a role and a script. Each scenario took a predictable course. He replicated this scenario in school and at work with punitive teachers and bosses. And he always told himself these events were his fault. Notice that Ken experienced betrayal by known and trusted people, that the family's reactions were extreme, and that there was a predictable cycle of events in which his role was very clear—he received the punishments for the excess of the family. He and Charlie Brown both knew their roles. Those roles support traumatic bonding.

One other trait was present. The roles in the family could quickly reverse. His mom, who ordered the beatings, would also rescue him from his brothers. His wife, who was trying to rescue him from the insanity of the family, would attack him for not being stronger. His brothers would befriend him after the attacks and plot against Mom. All of this added to the volatility and intensity of the family. Which brings us to the last major source of strength for trauma bonds.

WHEN THE ROLES OF VICTIM, VICTIMIZER AND RESCUER SWITCH

Role switching is common in betrayal bonding. Domestic abuse serves as an excellent example. Police are often very slow to respond to domestic abuse situations; they have learned that can be extremely dangerous for the officer. Here is how it works:

The 911 call comes. The intervening officer arrives at the scene. His first priority is to restrain the perpetrator so he can gain control of the situation. When the officer attempts to secure the perpetrator, the battered spouse attacks him. And who separates them, looking like the epitome of calm and reason? The original perpetrator. This dynamic routinely injures or kills. It is the same dynamic that worked in Ken's family.

Psychiatrist Stephen Karpman identified this switch in what clinicians call the Karpman triangle. There are three critical roles involved: (1) exploited or violated the victim; (2) the victimizer who exploits or violates the victim; and (3) the rescuer who wants to stop the transgression. In the case of domestic abuse, the intervening officer is the rescuer. The officer becomes the victim when the battered spouse, who becomes the victimizer, attacks him. The perpetrator then becomes the rescuer.[12] Figure 4.3 graphically shows the interaction of the three roles.

Traumatic bonding thrives when the system reverses its victim, victimizer and rescuer roles. It makes the betrayal exponential because it adds insecurity, intensity and complexity to the situation. The cycles, the uniqueness and the reactivity in traumatic bonding become even more volatile, all of which add to the anxiety and the terror.

Remember the fundamental premise: Attachment deepens with terror. This occurs not only in domestic abuse; it happens in incest and sexual misconduct when the victim threatens exposure and becomes aggressive with the victimizer for the purpose of exploitation. When congressman Ryan went to save the victims in Jonestown, they killed him. In Stockholm, the hostages were critical and abusive toward the rescuers. In the story at the beginning of this chapter, when Don and Jan were betraying Phil, the bank officers, in rescuing Phil, opened themselves to substantial lawsuits and federal penalties for betraying client confidence. These role reversals are what keep the dramatic momentum going. They are the stuff of which soap operas are made.

Figure 4.3. The Karpman Triangle

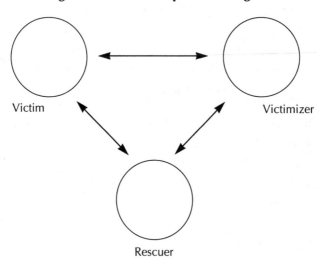

Further, all three roles (victim, victimizer, rescuer) have important similarities. All three roles originate from shame and self-doubt. All three positions stem from a sense of being defective and unworthy. People in these dramas are never confident that anyone will fulfill their needs. The victim allies with the perpetrator in the hope of gaining acceptance and meeting her needs. The victimizer so fears that his needs will not be met that he feels he has to deceive and exploit the victim. And the rescuer is trying to secure a place by being heroic, hoping that if he goes to this extreme the others will recognize his needs and meet them.

Ironically, all three roles identify with the victim in the other. The victim believes the perpetrator's story of victimization. The perpetrator identifies with the victim by making the promise—knowing exactly what the victim wants. The rescuer wants to protect the victim since the rescuer has an abuse history as well. The net result is that they all obsess about one other: The victim obsesses about the perpetrator, the perpetrator obsesses about the victim, and the rescuer obsesses about the crisis.

In each role the participants use magical thinking. The victim is naïve in repeatedly trusting that things will change. For Charlie Brown to think that Lucy is actually going to hold the ball for him is not logical, given the history. The victimizer is naïve in thinking the true intent will not emerge. Sooner or later the truth will come out. And the rescuer is naïve in thinking the rescue will actually work.

All three positions represent boundary failure. Victims fail to protect themselves; victimizers fail to limit themselves; and rescuers fail to define themselves. They become enmeshed with others when they're caught up in a crisis. They lose their sense of self. Because of this, their personal boundaries become too elastic.

There is a grandiosity in all this. Victims are grandiose in seeing themselves as beneficiaries of the promise; victimizers are grandiose in telling the story that contains the promise; and rescuers are grandiose by believing one intervention can do away with the past. Figure 4.4 summarizes these dimensions for all three positions.

The bottom line: The reason a person can be in all three roles in the same traumatic relationship is that the person shares the commonalities listed in the chart in figure 4.4. All victimizers need to see that they also play victim and rescuer; all victims need to see how they rescue and victimize; all rescuers need to understand their own motivation for helping lest they become victims or worse, victimizers; and anyone who has been part of a betrayal bond needs to understand how all role reversals intensify insane loyalties. It is the history of all great bonding conflicts: the Hatfields and the McCoys, the Montagues and the Capulets of *Romeo and Juliet* fame, the wars between Mafia families—betrayal and counter-betrayal.

At the conclusion of this chapter is an exercise on your conflict history. As in earlier exercises, this activity will help you

Figure 4.4. Commonalities for Victim, Victimizer and Rescuer

DIMENSION	VICTIM	VICTIMIZER	RESCUER
Shame	doubts personal value	doubts personal value	doubts personal value
Needs deficit	allies with perpetrator to meet needs	deceives and violates victim to meet needs	becomes heroic to meet needs
Abuse identification	sees victim in the perpetrator's story	identifies with victim in promise	wants to protect victim in others
Obsession	with perpetrator	with victim	with crisis
Magical thinking	naïve in repeatedly trusting	naïve in thinking he or she will not be caught	naïve in thinking rescue will work
Boundary failure	failure to protect self	failure to limit self	failure to define self

form a complete picture of your own relationships. Again, keep a record of your reactions to completing the inventory, as it will be of great assistance to you shortly.

CONFLICT INVENTORY

Sometimes we can learn much about ourselves by studying the conflicts that we have had. List ten people below with whom you have had a significant conflict. Note what relationship you had with the person. After each person, write a two- to three-sentence description of your primary coping strategies. In what ways did you strategize to deal with the problems in the relationship. After each person check the appropriate boxes as to whether you participated in the role of victim, victimizer or rescuer.

NAME OF PERSON	PRIMARY COPING STRATEGIES	ROLES PLAYED (check each)
Example: A. John B. (my brother)	I was cold and withdrawn. Sometimes I would get angry and make threats. I tried to get his wife as an ally. Also, I told everything I knew to my parents so they would force him to see the light. I saw his boss in the store and told him what was going on.	(X) victim (X) victimizer (X) rescuer
Example: B. Bill (my husband)	I would agree to calm him down and try to keep the peace. I would let him get his way until things got too awful. Then I would have a temper tantrum and throw things.	(X) victim (X) victimizer ( ) rescuer
1.		( ) victim ( ) victimizer ( ) rescuer
2.		( ) victim ( ) victimizer ( ) rescuer
3.		( ) victim ( ) victimizer ( ) rescuer
4.		( ) victim ( ) victimizer ( ) rescuer

NAME OF PERSON	PRIMARY COPING STRATEGIES	ROLES PLAYED (check each)
5.		( ) victim ( ) victimizer ( ) rescuer
6.		( ) victim ( ) victimizer ( ) rescuer
7.		( ) victim ( ) victimizer ( ) rescuer
8.		( ) victim ( ) victimizer ( ) rescuer
9.		( ) victim ( ) victimizer ( ) rescuer
10.		( ) victim ( ) victimizer ( ) rescuer

What We Have Learned So Far . . .

We need to stop and take stock of how far we have come in understanding trauma bonds. Here is a summary of the principles we know so far.

Trauma bonds are strongest when:

there is danger

there is no escape or there is no perceived way out

there is seduction and betrayal

there is a supporting script or compelling story and a deep desire for it to be true

there is an abuse of power

there is an abuse of intimacy

there is an abuse of spirit

there is a desire to rescue

there is a failure to protect yourself

there is an inability to meet personal needs

there are repetitive cycles of abuse

the victim and victimizer believe in their own uniqueness

high intensity is mistaken for intimacy

there is confusion about love

there are increasing amounts of fear

children are faced with terror

there is also a history of abuse

exploitation involves trusted family members or trusted family friends and it lasts a long time

the community, family or social structure reacts in the extremes

there are familiar roles and scripts

the roles of victim, victimizer and rescuer switch

Write in your journal about your reactions as you look at this list. How many of these conditions fit for you? Does it help you to understand how you own relationships?

5

WHAT IS THE PATH OF AWARENESS?

For Anita Hill, "family" began as her relationship with [Clarence] Thomas, who was not only a colleague, but a boss and a "father figure" to her and others. Thomas spoke of his supervisees as being like his "children," and how he often had fatherly feelings for them. For such a "father" to betray his "child" is common in our world of unhealthy families. Anita Hill also has a greater family—in her workplace, and then finally in her government, where she and we encountered the unhealthy family of the Senate and its Judiciary Committee. And this Committee had a secret, likely only one among many more secrets, that it tried to keep from itself and the nation.

CHARLES WHITFIELD[1]

The range of what we think and do is limited by what we fail to notice and because we fail to notice that we fail to notice there is little we can do to change until we notice how failing to notice shapes our thoughts and desires.

R. D. LAING

111

"Exactly!" Tom's therapist exclaimed. "You don't feel loving, you feel bonded!" Tom and his therapist, Sam, had just spent the last hour of therapy going round and round. Tom had been divorced from his ex-spouse for over four years. They had three children together and a nightmare for a relationship. His ex-wife, Barbara, had been manipulative, cruel to him and the children, and very abusive in her frequent attacks of rage. Tom persisted in being calm and giving despite all this. His therapist was pushing him as to why. Tom had said he did not love her but somehow he connected to her. Sam was working to help him understand that he had a trauma bond.

In part, his therapist made sense. Barbara had always been volatile. Their courtship had regular episodes of angry dramatic exits alternated with incredible displays of devotion by Barbara. Sometimes Tom thought he was coerced into the marriage, although he could not quite put the idea into words. For Barbara, Tom's hesitancy to get married was not acceptable. It was going to happen. She waged a campaign to mobilize the good will of everyone around Tom. What they did not see were her outbreaks of rage. Finally she got pregnant and that was it.

About four months into the marriage, Barbara had an affair with her supervisor. From that point, things started unraveling. She started a campaign about how bad a husband Tom was. Consequently, Tom ended up defending himself, which angered him. Barbara had the affair and he was the one who was defensive! When he was ready to leave she love-bombed him and they ended up with a second child. Six years into the marriage and three children later, he could not stand it anymore, and they separated. The divorce talks were interminable, and Tom spent much of every day coping with the chaos Barbara created. Sam was helping Tom to see that he had not really left at all.

Tom could not figure it out. He did not feel loving toward her. He was no longer attracted to her. He did not respect her, nor did he did trust her. Their history together verified over and over again that she would go to any lengths to get what she wanted and present a positive image to the outside world. She deliberately lied in therapy. However, when the children came to therapy and corroborated Tom's reality in front of the therapists, she looked contrite and aghast. Once out of the therapy office, she threw a fit before they got to the car. A reign of terror started, which let everybody know that what had just happened was not to happen again. For openers, she refused to let the children go to therapy again. Then there were outright lies. She told Tom's parents and sisters stories that were far from reality.

The lies and the raging continued. Given this history, Tom could not understand how, or why, he was still so involved with her. He admitted to Sam that at times he felt over-whelmed with anger and despaired that his life was ruined. As long as he was actively a father to the children, he would have to pay the price.

Tom paid in many ways. He paid financially. His attorney in the divorce was upset because Tom conceded many points that he did not have to. He had some profound need to be "fair," which to outsiders looked absolutely self-destructive. After read-ing a draft of the divorce decree, Tom's secretary joked with him by asking if she could be married to him even for a little while.

Tom also paid in time. Barbara was on the phone three or four times a day—complaining, raging, cajoling or asking for help or advice.

He paid in disruption. Barbara moved into a house two blocks from Tom's. The idea was to make it more convenient for the kids. The net effect was that Tom could not have a meal with his children or spend an evening with them without Barbara having some reason to show up, often with her latest man in tow.

Sam pressed Tom to accept that this chaos was not about Barbara alone. True, she did awful things, but Tom participated as well. The two of them had a deep negative attachment for each other. Tom was hooked into her as much as she was into him. Sam made a statement that to Tom was like a Zen koan: "Barbara is no longer your wife and yet she is not your 'ex' either." "So what is she then?" snapped Tom. Sam smiled back and said, "Barbara is your addiction."

THE PATH OF DENIAL

From 1985 to 1990, I directed a team of researchers who followed the recovery of over a thousand sex addicts. This group had a number of significant characteristics, beyond their sex addiction, that made them important to study. First, they had multiple addictions: alcoholism and drug addiction (42 percent); eating disorders, including anorexia (38 percent); and other forms of addictive compulsion, including work, spending and gambling. Further, they had histories of trauma and abuse: sexual abuse (81 percent), physical abuse (72 percent) and emotional abuse (97 percent). Finally, many of them reported the type of traumatic bonding I've described in this book. From the data collected and with the help of a university computer, we were able to reconstruct the process by which trauma impacts people. We began to understand the confusion and denial people like Tom have about their relationships. More important, we discerned the process by which people restored their lives. I learned a lot from the project. In fact, it started me in the direction of researching and developing the material for this book.

Here is what we learned. For most people, there was some original trauma. Remember, this does not have to be some earth-shattering event. It can be as simple as neglect, or it can be witnessing something traumatic such as incest or domestic abuse. When that original trauma occurs, we begin to see the first signs of compulsive behavior. Compulsive masturbation, for example, was common for many of the sex addicts in our study. Other forms of compulsion emerged as well. An abused child will learn, for the sake of her own survival, to focus on the emotional well-being of the abusing caregiver. The child will become "expert" at noticing and responding to the moods of her abuser. The child may, for example, become expert at caregiving as a way to soothe the parent, or may feel compelled to become compliant as a way to lower the anxiety of the abuser. Yet another option exists, given that abuse intensifies the child's attachment to the abuser. The child may learn how to endure pain in order to maintain the bond with the caregiver. These "compelling" patterns form a working model for how the child will later deal with significant people in her life. As an adult, the working model becomes the template for all-important relationships.

Tom was classic in this sense. He had an alcoholic father known for his rages. He remembers the screaming as his mother barricaded herself in the bedroom. He remembers the ambulance when she was injured. When he was eight, his father joined Alcoholics Anonymous and the fighting stopped, but he was always afraid of his father's temper. He was also very good at consoling his mother. To use Sam's words, he was one of the world's best "at walking on eggshells and comforting the wounded." It was only after Sam and a clinic hypnotist helped Tom talk about the feelings he had as he watched these events that Tom accepted his internal terror.

Victims acclimatize to the terror. They distort, transform, reinterpret, dissociate, distance, repress, disown, or use any of a number of strategies to accommodate their reality. We call this denial. They also can have traumatic amnesia, which means there is no conscious recall of specific events. For example, Tom's brother and sister told him of specific events they witnessed of which he had no memory. Similarly, Tom told them of events that he was absolutely sure happened to the three of them, that his siblings could not remember. That is when Tom first understood what Sam meant by repression.

Children are presented with what trauma researcher David Calof has described as the "universal bind." Do not see, hear, sense, feel or address what is real. Instead, accept what is unreal and proscribed in the interest of your survival. Disbelieve the obvious and accept the improbable.[2] The bind is that the child is presented with only two options: (1) be overwhelmed with terror and not able to function, or (2) distort reality to survive. Because of the bind, distorting reality becomes part of the "working model" eventually used in adult relationships. Therapists Blizard and Bluhm describe it this way:

> These defenses are highly adaptive in childhood, because they permit the child to survive in an abusive family. In adulthood the defenses become maladaptive, because they prevent the survivor from accurately perceiving the presence or absence of abuse. By permitting the adult survivor to maintain a relationship with someone who resembles the original abuser, these defenses perpetuate the cycle of abuse.[3]

In Tom's case, Barbara combined the angry violence and intimidation of his dad with the compelling sadness of his mom. While an irresistible combination, Tom had to make up a narrative or story that made sense to him in order to stay connected to Barbara, but to outsiders his explanations were bizarre distortions and rationalizations. Combine this with Barbara's fictions and distortions, and reality became very elusive for anyone looking in from the outside.

With denial and repression in place, all the trauma solutions are available in the service of the trauma bond. Reactivity, arousal, blocking, splitting, abstinence, shame and trauma repetition can be accomplished in the context of the relationship.

Reactivity comes with constant chaos, involvement and betrayal. There is always something to induce the cycles of old to activate the victim, victimizer and rescuer scenarios.

Arousal surges in the relationship with high risk, intensity and sometimes violent sex. Anger, fear and anxiety create a neurochemical cascade that makes sane relationships boring.

Blocking occurs when there is the honeymoon or "I have pushed you too far" phase. Seductive and pleasing efforts to "make up for it" are calming and provide temporary relief.

Splitting happens when the victim dissociates from the chaos or from obsessing about the partner. Internal dialogues with your partner would be an example.

Abstinence manifests in many ways, including the obvious: staying in the relationship without needs being met, or worse, living in deprivation because the chaos prevents you from taking care of yourself, so martyrdom seems functional.

Shame appears in the form of despair about yourself, in feeling defective because the victim has absorbed the shame of the perpetrator (carried shame), and in believing in your unworthiness.

Repetition cycles the "working model" of how relationships should work over and over again. Each recycle repeats the victimization of the past.

In short, you have an addictive relationship that results in compulsive involvement and compulsive relationship patterns. For Tom, being with Barbara put in place all the paths that people use addictively.

In addition, notice that the addictive relationship is woven with other addictive compulsive behaviors. Core to this process are: alcohol and drug abuse; sex addiction; eating disorders; compulsive working, spending and gambling; and the compulsive seeking of high-risk situations (including violence and arrest). Very seldom will you find traumatic bonding without other addictions woven into the pattern on somebody's, if not everybody's, part. Conversely, seldom do you find addictions of any type without vulnerability to traumatic bonding. A complex constellation of out-of-control relationships and behaviors emerges. It's a cycle that results in a self-perpetuating system.

Sooner or later this system gathers enough momentum that a life crisis occurs. Something so bad happens that the victim can no longer simply go forward. Forgetting about the past and coping with the day is not enough. Those who have the courage decide to change, whatever the cost; it literally takes that kind of resolve to make the change. Figure 5.1 summarizes the role trauma plays in the evolution of the life crisis.

Figure 5.1. Role of Trauma in a Life Crisis

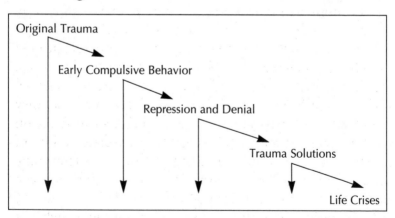

In figure 5.1, note that the development of the survivor starts with the original trauma and then proceeds to early compulsive behavior. This behavior may have a role in helping with the repression and denial that come into play. As the full force of the various trauma options becomes available, the chaos escalates to the point of life crisis. The arrows graphically show the sequence of the progression. Also notice that there is an arrow that points down. This represents how each dimension progresses. The original perpetrator may continue abusing. Those early compulsive behaviors will persist. The denial and repression continue and expand, as will the traumatic solutions they enable. All of this continues until it crashes under its own weight. The survivor can no longer keep up with all of it.

THE PATH OF AWARENESS

By reconstructing the path from the original trauma to the life crisis, we gained an important insight into recovery. People in our study recovered in stages, and the order of their recovery was almost the reverse of how people got into their life crises. Most had to experience some type of intervention to get out of the trauma-based system. If they were addicted to alcohol or gambling, they had to start a recovery program around that illness. If they were hooked into a destructive relationship, they had to do something about it. If they were dissociating, stuck in deprivation behaviors or immersed in shame, they would seek treatment for it. To start, they had to focus on the trauma solutions, identifying the immediate source of the chaos. Their recovery was akin to putting up a tent in the wind—some pegs have to go in the ground before you can anchor the tent and raise the poles.

These early interventions create confusion about what is real. The survivors, in beginning these initial changes, also start to accept that the rationalization and distortions they have used or believed were part of the problem. And they were confused by that. Remember, a survivor has been asked to disbelieve the obvious and accept the improbable. After the intervention, survivors were unsure of what reality really was. This created the window for the next stage—the stage in which denial and repression break. When survivors stop using the dysfunctional solutions they have used (i.e., high-risk behavior, medicating or anesthetizing, repeating the event), they can expect that:

> memories of previous abuse will return
>
> they will have intense reactions to what they do remember
>
> they will have an expanded understanding of what happened in the past
>
> they will see continuing aspects of those abusive patterns now
>
> they will know how high the cost has been
>
> they will be very fearful of what this means for them and their lives

After the intervention, those participating in the study asked several questions: What if this is all true? What does this mean about me? About my family? What will happen now if I say this out loud? How will people react? Will it be worse if I admit the truth? Is it safer to hide? As you've read this book, you may have asked yourself some of those same questions.

If you understand that this fearful reaction is the beginning of grief, it helps. Whenever there is significant loss—whether individually or collectively—the stages of human grieving are quite predictable. First, there is denial—"This cannot be true!" Then there is fear—"What if it is true?" This is followed by anger—"This is unfair!" Anger is followed by the wrenching pain of loss—"This hurts too much to bear." Finally, there is acceptance and an attempt to derive some meaning out of all that happened.

There are several things that make it different for survivors. First, grief is delayed. Most grief cycles begin with a current loss, such as the death of a loved one. Survivors have not been able to acknowledge the pain that has been accumulating. It is somewhat akin to running in front of a growing avalanche for years and never being more than a few inches in front of it. When you stop, the avalanche overwhelms you. When you no longer have the cushion of the trauma solutions, the pain envelops you all at once.

Second, the initial trauma may have distorted the relationship template used as an adult. The result is that survivors have a vulnerability most people do not have. They often are not able to discern when someone is being exploitive or abusive toward them. This interferes with their sense of loss, their outrage and their pain.

Third, most people plunged into grief can be public about their loss. If a loved one dies in an auto accident, there is no mystery as to why the family members hurt. But when the loss is shrouded in pledges of secrecy and in shame and betrayal, getting support will require incredible vulnerability: "How could I have been so foolish? So trusting and accepting?" Worse, talking about the loss means disloyalty within the abusive system. Anger can help break the loyalty of the betrayal bond. For survivors, the typical anger at God most people in grief experience is coupled with anger toward the victimizer. This anger becomes an empowering emotion that helps to break the secrecy and dissolve the insane loyalties.

Finally, most people grieve because the loss is painful. Survivors must add another dimension to that pain. It starts when they realize that the people who abused them also were abused. Perhaps the abuse may even go back many generations. Survivors move beyond this realization to a new level of integrity when they acknowledge that they have also abused others. Maybe they did not do the same things, but they still victimized others. They are part of an unbroken chain, which can be incredibly painful to admit. We call this *victimization consciousness,* which means the victim understands the whole picture. She now grasps and accepts the whole complex series of relationships, solutions to trauma, and accumulated loss. With that acceptance comes a new sense of peace.

Figure 5.2. Awareness of Victimization Consciousness

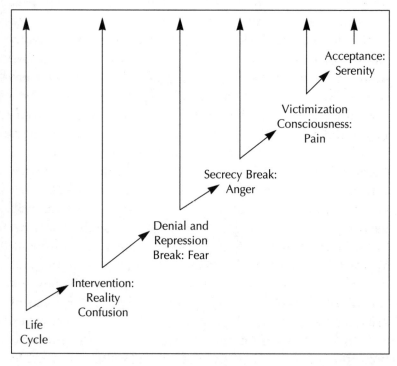

Figure 5.2 graphically represents this process of awareness and understanding. It is the reverse path of the denial that protects the abusive system and its web of solutions to the trauma. The arrows in the figure show the order in which things occur. Note also the arrows indicating that each phase of this path

READER/CUSTOMER CARE SURVEY

We care about your opinions. Please take a moment to fill out this Reader Survey card and mail it back to us.

As a special **"thank you"** we'll send you exciting news about interesting books and a valuable **Gift Certificate.**

Please PRINT using ALL CAPS

First Name [   ] MI. [   ] Last Name [   ]

Address [   ]

City [   ] ST [   ] Zip [   ]

Phone # ([   ]) [   ] — [   ]   Fax # ([   ]) [   ] — [   ]

Email [   ]

(1) Gender:
___ Female   ___ Male

(2) Age:
___ 12 or under   ___ 40-59
___ 13-19   ___ 60+
___ 20-39

(3) Marital Status
___ Married
___ Single
___ Divorced/Widowed

(4) Did you receive this book as a gift?
___ Yes   ___ No

(5) How many Health Communications books have you bought or read?
___ 1   ___ 2-4   ___ 5+

(6) How did you find out about this book?
Please fill in ONE.
1) ___ Recommendation
2) ___ Store Display
3) ___ Bestseller List
4) ___ Online
5) ___ Advertisement
6) ___ Catalog/Mailing
7) ___ Interview/Review (TV, Radio, Print)

(7) Where do you usually buy books?
Please fill in your top TWO choices.
1) ___ Bookstore
2) ___ Religious Bookstore
3) ___ Online
4) ___ Book Club/Mail Order
5) ___ Price Club (Costco, Sam's Club, etc.)
6) ___ Retail Store (Target, Wal-Mart, etc.)

(9) What subjects do you enjoy reading about most? Rank only *FIVE*. Use 1 for your favorite, 2 for second favorite, etc.

	1	2	3	4	5
1) Parenting/Family	○	○	○	○	○
2) Relationships	○	○	○	○	○
3) Recovery/Addictions	○	○	○	○	○
4) Health/Nutrition	○	○	○	○	○
5) Christianity	○	○	○	○	○
6) Spirituality/Inspiration	○	○	○	○	○
7) Business Self-Help	○	○	○	○	○
8) Teen Issues	○	○	○	○	○
9) Sports	○	○	○	○	○

(14) What attracts you most to a book?
(Please rank 1-4 in order of preference.)

	1	2	3	4
1) Title	○	○	○	○
2) Cover Design	○	○	○	○
3) Author	○	○	○	○
4) Content	○	○	○	○

TAPE IN MIDDLE; DO NOT STAPLE

BUSINESS REPLY MAIL
FIRST-CLASS MAIL PERMIT NO 45 DEERFIELD BEACH, FL

POSTAGE WILL BE PAID BY ADDRESSEE

HEALTH COMMUNICATIONS, INC.
3201 SW 15TH STREET
DEERFIELD BEACH FL 33442-9875

FOLD HERE

Comments:

continues. You do not simply go through the phases and finish. Survivors will continue to make connections with their memories and their current circumstances.

Each stage of awareness will go through the process. With time, the survivor will acquire the skills to process through these realizations more rapidly. It will become more manageable: This is a promise.

It is important to examine each phase of the path of awareness from a traumatic bonding perspective.

DENIAL AND REPRESSION

Let's summarize the problem: Adults who are trauma-bonded to people who are harmful to them believe they have made that choice. Everyone around them can see how compulsive the relationship is except the person involved. The trauma-bonded person has also constructed a story that explains the initial involvement and rationalizes the continued involvement. The story has powerful reasons for what happened and powerful hopes for change. Sometimes this story is a variant of the perpetrator's story of promise, but sometimes not. The critical factor is that this scenario, with its embedded conclusions, came from the victim, and for that reason it is particularly difficult to overcome.

In 1942, Anna Freud described this process as "identification with the aggressor." She meant that the victim will start to perceive the world from the point of view of the aggressor. Since then we have acquired a greater understanding of what goes into traumatic bonding. We know it has a profound neurochemical impact, and it creates a working model for other relationships. We understand the complex web of addictive and family systems that preserves this "identification." Yet at the core of the bonding is a story.

To breach the denial, the victim needs to step outside of the story and see it as others see it. In part that is how a therapist, therapy group or support group can be helpful. It requires, however, courage and willingness. A helpful exercise is to write a brief narrative of your life story as if it were the story of someone else. Usually you start as if it were a fairy tale: "Once there was a little girl (boy) . . ." In writing, most victims start to have compassion for the character in the story that is themselves. They begin to see the faulty logic their character has used. When read by the victims to a support or therapy group, there is often a profound shift in the victims as they start to acknowledge the pain. They would not have been able to achieve that understanding without looking differently at the story. Instructions for writing the story follow.

When Tom did this exercise, it was life-changing. One of the toughest parts for him to acknowledge was that as a man, he was a victim. He told Sam, his therapist, that he always thought that as a man he should be in charge. It was extremely hard for him to admit that he was easily manipulated and that he did not protect himself well. Further, he felt afraid often because it always seemed that Barbara was a move or two ahead of him. Those admissions came hard for a man who was supposed to be in charge.

WRITE THE STORY

This assignment asks that you write your own story in your journal, but write as if it happened to someone else. Use third-person pronouns in your description: "Once there was a girl and she . . ." It may help you to visualize it as a movie or a fairy tale. Limit yourself to 750 words or less (about three pages). Focus on how the character in the story is thinking and feeling. You may wish to draw a picture or two with crayons to illustrate the story. After you have finished, do the following:

With your therapist or group, read the story out loud and show the pictures.

If you think of this as happening to someone else, what feelings do you have for the character?

What do you wish to tell the character?

Write in your journal about the realities you have not been willing to examine.

Record any patterns you see emerging throughout your life.

Record any common profiles of persons you recognize.

What Tom and other victims learn is that compulsive relationship patterns start early. They start as survival strategies for the child, but for the adult they become imprisoning patterns. Trauma specialists observe the following common compulsive relationship patterns:[4]

1. Compulsive Helplessness—The child is so focused on the adult and the abuse, she does not learn to master her environment or take care of herself well. Therapists refer to this uninvolved state as *learned helplessness*, or inattention. They irritate others because they do not notice what needs to be done. Adults with this pattern face constant chaos because they do not act for themselves and do not provide their basic needs. They seem oblivious until there is a crisis.

2. Compulsive Focus on the Abuser—For survival's sake, the child becomes an "expert" on the abuser. What the child wants or needs becomes subservient to the caregiver's moods. Thus the child loses the sense of self and identifies with the source of fear. As an adult, the person will obsess about anyone with power over her and do whatever she can to control what happens.

3. Compulsive Self-Reliance—As an alternative strategy to the previous two options, the child will become excessively self-reliant. No needs are expressed. No help is asked or accepted. All affection and closeness are avoided. As an adult the victim will use self-sufficiency as a defense against needing others.

4. Compulsive Caregiving—Priority is placed on the needs of the others, with feelings of martyrdom and resentment resulting. Self-sacrifice goes to the extreme. Care is supplied whether requested or not, whether needed or not. As adults, victims become burdensome and easily exploitable.

5. Compulsive Care-Seeking—Problems are presented so that care will be received. Relationships are defined by those who can supply assistance. The victim expects others to assume responsibility for major areas of life. The only way anyone gets close to the victim is by providing help. As adults, victims will always present the latest problem as a reason to have a relationship.

6. Compulsive Rejection—Extreme negative reactions result from perceived unavailability of or lack of response by the caregiver or abuser. Often a generalized anger occurs on the principle of "I will reject you before you have a chance to reject me." Such emotional violence simply echoes a violent home life. In adults, this emotional volatility can become a way of victimizing others.

7. Compulsive Compliance—This is a placating stance in which being extremely agreeable provides protection from more abuse. No wish is challenged. Resistance is token. No boundaries exist. As adults, these people commit to things they do not wish to do, provide information they should not provide, and do things that are self-destructive, uncomfortable or dangerous simply because someone asked them.

8. Compulsive Identification with Others—This person can easily be sold a "bill of goods." He or she has instant sympathy for even the most patent lies, tales of insanity, stories of hardship and seduction strategies. Victims may even have the capacity to see through the seduction, but in the presence of the perpetrator they get carried away by the story. Their gullibility produces personal loss and constant chaos. They are especially irritating to others because they will never negotiate on their own behalf.

9. Compulsive Reality Distortion—The victim will persist in not seeing abuse as abuse. Excuses, rationalization, minimization and other defenses combine to allow the endurance of more pain and exploitation. In part, this comes from the deep wish that the story or promise of the perpetrator be true. In adults, it means ignoring the obvious.

10. Compulsive Abuse Seeking—The victim sets up relationships to repeat the same patterns of abuse. This creates familiar binds, neurochemistry and coping strategies. For a relationship to work, it must comply with the original abuse scenario. What can vary is the amount of risk and intensity. Adults may combine a number of abuse scenarios to get the desired effect.

At the core of every addiction is compulsive behavior. Compulsion means that you exhibit the behavior even though you know it is self-destructive. You cannot stop it on your own. Traumatic bonding is essentially a compulsive relationship with very definite patterns of compulsive behavior.

For successful recovery, the victim has to be able to break through denial and see the compulsive patterns for what they are. I've provided a compulsive relationship self-assessment as a way to start facing the reality of those compulsive patterns. It is structured on the ten dimensions described above. On those dimensions that you rate yourself high, you will be asked to describe events in childhood in which that dimension was evident. The goal of the exercise is to help you see each dimension as a coping strategy you needed at that time. Next to each of those childhood examples you will be asked to record a parallel adult event in which the same behavior is dysfunctional.

It is certainly possible for a person with little or none of these compulsive patterns in childhood to experience trauma bonding as an adult. As an adult, some situations are so terrifying that they can immediately precipitate these compulsive behaviors and alter a person's life. If you are in that situation, simply focus on the adult examples.

It may also happen as a result of this and the previous exercise that you will remember traumatic events you had forgotten. Expect traumatic repression to lift as you work on these issues. Simply record them and add them to your understanding. It means the process is working. You will have feelings about them, which you should also record. But also note that your awareness is expanding, which is good news.

Please complete the compulsive relationship self-assessment before you continue reading this book.

COMPULSIVE RELATIONSHIP
SELF-ASSESSMENT

Complete the following self-assessment by assigning yourself a number between one and ten in each compulsive dimension. A rating of one, on a scale of ten, would mean there was little or none of that behavior present. By contrast, a score of ten would mean that the behavior was constant (a daily experience). Once you have completed the scales, note those you have rated five or above. Next to these higher rated scales, record a childhood event that describes how you coped with the compulsivity. Then record an adult event that shows the same pattern.

DIMENSIONS OF COMPULSIVITY	CHILDHOOD EVENT (COPING STRATEGY)	ADULT EVENT (DYSFUNCTIONAL PATTERN)
Example: A. Compulsive Self-Reliance 1 2 3 4 5 6 7 ⑧ 9 10	I refused any help with my homework from teachers, parents or anybody. The result was that I often did poorly in school.	I insisted on doing my taxes myself and got audited. It took three years to get out of trouble with the IRS.
Example: B. Compulsive Compliance 1 2 3 4 5 6 ⑦ 8 9 10	I would rub Dad's back and sleep in his bed when I really hated doing it, but I feared I would be beaten.	I would sleep with Jim and give him a massage just to calm things down after he hit me.
1. Compulsive Helplessness 1 2 3 4 5 6 7 8 9 10		
2. Compulsive Focus on the Abuser 1 2 3 4 5 6 7 8 9 10		
3. Compulsive Self-Reliance 1 2 3 4 5 6 7 8 9 10		
4. Compulsive Caregiving 1 2 3 4 5 6 7 8 9 10		

DIMENSIONS OF COMPULSIVITY	CHILDHOOD EVENT (COPING STRATEGY)	ADULT EVENT (DYSFUNCTIONAL PATTERN)
5. Compulsive Care-Seeking 1 2 3 4 5 6 7 8 9 10		
6. Compulsive Rejection 1 2 3 4 5 6 7 8 9 10		
7. Compulsive Compliance 1 2 3 4 5 6 7 8 9 10		
8. Compulsive Identification with Others 1 2 3 4 5 6 7 8 9 10		
9. Compulsive Reality Distortion 1 2 3 4 5 6 7 8 9 10		
10. Compulsive Abuse Seeking 1 2 3 4 5 6 7 8 9 10		

What reactions do you have to seeing a profile of the areas of compulsive behavior in your relationships? Record these reactions in your journal. In scales you rated as eight, generate a list of examples from both childhood and adult life so you are very clear as to how the patterns affect you.

TRAUMA BONDS AND CODEPENDENCY

Those readers who are familiar with addictions might wonder what the difference is between codependency and traumatic bonding. An additional risk could be that, out of denial, some might categorize a trauma bond as codependency. We can define codependency as an obsessive attachment to one or more addicted people. Family members who live with alcoholics, sex addicts, compulsive gamblers, compulsive overeaters, drug addicts or those with other addictive disorders develop a diagnosable set of compulsive characteristics that parallel many of the behaviors present in betrayal bonding.[5] Some of the most commonly mentioned characteristics of codependents are:

collusion with the addicts in the form of covering up for them, keeping secrets about them or joining with them in their addictive activities

obsession with the addict and addictive behavior, including attempting to catch the addict in lies, focusing on the addict to the degree of neglect of self and family, and being preoccupied with the addict and the addict's activities

denial of reality about the addict to the extent of over-extending themselves to avoid the problem and believing they can change the addict

emotional turmoil that makes life a roller coaster of problems and chaos, and creates incredible intensity manipulative in the drive to control the addict, including frequent use of martyrdom (victim), hero (rescuer) and avenger (victimizer) roles

    excessive responsibility in a variety of ways, including feeling responsible for the addict's behavior and making themselves indispensable in order to prevent abandonment

    compromise of self to meet the addict's demands, thereby acting against their own morals, values and beliefs

    self-righteous judgment, which often results in dramatic scenes and punitive, vengeful behavior

    severe reactivity, including overreaction and under-reaction to everyday situations such as avoiding sex and other forms of deprivation[5]

Parallels do exist between trauma bonding and codependency because to live with an active addict is often traumatic. For the most part, the addiction field has not incorporated all the trauma research that documents how people grow closer to their abusers in the face of trauma. Yet it is clear that many codependents are also trauma-bonded. The converse is also true. The trauma field has not really addressed issues surrounding addiction, let alone codependency. Yet addiction in its many forms is one of the principal solutions used by survivors to cope with their lives. And most trauma-bonded persons, whether as children or adults, are involved with an abuser who has one or more addictions.

Differences do exist, however. Here is one way to make sense of it. Codependent obsession is with the addictive process. The reactivity is to any form of the addiction with which codependents have had to suffer. So spouses and children of alcoholics might think anyone who drinks excessively can be suspect. To use trauma language, it is a form of post-traumatic stress disorder. They were hurt by someone's abusive use of alcohol and they probably always will be reactive to it. In addition, some addicts are not particularly frightening. Family members may be sad and inappropriate in their behavior in an effort to help, but it is not the intense bonding and energy that occur with terror. Similarly, some people experience severe trauma bonds because of what was done to them and not because of a specific obsession with any addictive behavior.

Figure 5.3. Abuse and Addiction Populations

Figure 5.3 illustrates a way to look at two overlapping populations. One population focuses on the abuser. The other obsesses on the addiction. The two come together when the addict is also an abusive perpetrator. The overlap is extremely large, probably involving most of both populations. It is very important for codependents to understand the elements of trauma bonding. It is also critical for persons struggling with a traumatic bond to understand the nature of codependency. There is a rich set of resources and an extensive set of support groups that can help sort through denial and help manage reactive responses. Many survivors who have trouble with trauma bonding are addicts themselves. They can also participate in groups appropriate to the addictions they have.

THE TRANSITION FROM ANGER TO PAIN

Anger liberates the truth. But for many, true anger comes grudgingly. The loyalty rules still hold. You can ruin your life, and your abuser will shake his head in resignation. He will lock himself in a fortress of righteousness and denial, keeping at bay any realization of the role his abuse played in your life. Appropriate anger on the part of the victim can break through this denial and start a significant change process.

Yet there are all those rules about not upsetting people. "Children are to be seen and not heard." "If you cannot say something nice, don't say anything at all." Plus, there are all those sayings told to children to cajole them out of being upset: "Your face will freeze like that." "You are going to step on your lower lip and turn yourself inside out." Then there are family rules like "we keep our business in the family," which means "you better never tell anyone what happened."

The worst, however, are the rules of terror and betrayal. The worst betrayal is to let people know what happened. A parent might say, "If you talk about this, they will take me away." If you are a kid and already feel responsible for the abuse, this threat goes to your core: "What will happen to me if my parent is gone?" The most effective rules against anger are based in terror. Children know that to speak could mean a serious beating or even death. When you live with someone dangerous, you learn to keep the waters smooth. Thus there exists a web of rules against anger and a deep, almost pre-verbal, primitive fear of holding an abuser accountable.

Most victims need help expressing their anger. Therapists, therapy groups and support groups can help immensely in that process. You can write letters that may or may not be sent, or talk to an empty chair. These are two ways you can re-experience those early scenes and share the feelings with others now that you could not share when you were a child. If appropriate and safe, sharing the feelings with the abuser can often open up a path to healing and reconciliation. For those who are currently in a betrayal/trauma bond, anger becomes the source of resolve to change and to draw a line in the sand that says "no more."

One task that helps break through denial, overcome fear and develop a fierce resolve is to examine the costs. Often-times for addicts, this is a core part of what is called a First Step. In the First Step of Alcoholics Anonymous and other related Twelve-Step programs, the addicts and codependents look at both powerlessness (efforts made to stop the behavior) and unmanageability (what my behavior has cost me). A similar inventory, the Compulsive Relationship Consequences Inventory, has been provided for you around traumatic bonding. Before completing this inventory, go back to the journal and paperwork you have already completed, including your work on seduction and betrayal, your conflict survey and your Compulsive Relationship Self-Assessment. You will now be able to pull all that work together in terms of the impact these patterns have had on your life. Before proceeding to the remainder of the chapter, please complete the consequences inventory.

COMPULSIVE RELATIONSHIP CONSEQUENCES INVENTORY

Every person who has experienced compulsive relationship behavior has had consequences because of that behavior. You have probably had consequences. Sadly, people sometimes don't name what has happened to them as consequences, or they use their compulsive relationship behavior as a way to avoid feeling or admitting what has happened.

It is important that you look realistically at the consequences of your behavior in each of the categories listed. Put a check next to each of the things that you have experienced. In the space provided, record examples and dates if you can remember them.

Emotional Consequences: Examples and Dates

____ 1. Thoughts or feelings about committing suicide ____
_____

____ 2. Attempted suicide _____
_____

____ 3. Homicidal thoughts or feelings _____
_____

____ 4. Feelings of hopelessness and despair _____
_____

____ 5. Failed efforts to control your relationship _____
_____

____ 6. Feeling like you have two different lives—one public
and one secret _____
_____

____ 7. Depression, paranoia or fear of going insane _____
_____

____ 8. Loss of touch with reality _____
_____

____ 9. Loss of self-esteem _____
_____

____ 10. Loss of life goals _____
_____

____ 11. Acting against your own values and beliefs _____
_____

____ 12. Strong feelings of guilt and shame _____
_____

____ 13. Strong feelings of isolation and loneliness _____
_____

____ 14. Strong fears for your future _____
_____

___ 15. Emotional exhaustion _____

_____

___ 16. Other emotional consequences _____

_____

Physical Consequences

___ 1. Continuation of relationship despite the risk to your health _____

_____

___ 2. Extreme weight loss or gain _____

_____

___ 3. Physical problems (ulcers, high blood pressure, etc.)

_____

_____

___ 4. Physical injury or abuse by others _____

_____

___ 5. Involvement in potentially risky or dangerous situations _____

_____

___ 6. Vehicle accidents (automobile motorcycle, bicycle)

_____

_____

___ 7. Injury to yourself from your relationship _____

_____

___ 8. Sleep disturbances (not enough sleep, too much sleep) _____

_____

___ 9. Physical exhaustion _____

_____

____ 10. Other physical consequences related to your sexual behavior such as venereal disease, HIV/AIDS, bleeding, etc. _____

_____

Spiritual Consequences

____ 1. Feelings of spiritual emptiness _____

_____

____ 2. Feeling disconnected from yourself and the world

_____

_____

____ 3. Feeling abandoned by God or your Higher Power

_____

_____

____ 4. Anger at God or your Higher Power _____

_____

____ 5. Loss of faith in anything spiritual _____

_____

____ 6. Other spiritual consequences _____

_____

Consequences Related to Family

____ 1. Risking the loss of partner or spouse _____

_____

____ 2. Loss of partner or spouse _____

_____

____ 3. Increase in marital or relationship problems _____

_____

____ 4. Jeopardizing the well-being of your family _____

_____

___ 5. Loss of family's or partner's respect _____

___ 6. Increase in problems with your children _____

___ 7. Loss of your family of origin _____

___ 8. Other family or partnership consequences _____

Career and Educational Consequences

___ 1. Decrease in productivity in work _____

___ 2. Demotion at work _____

___ 3. Loss of coworkers' respect _____

___ 4. Loss of the opportunity to work in the career of your choice _____

___ 5. Failing grades in school _____

___ 6. Loss of educational opportunities _____

___ 7. Loss of business _____

___ 8. Forced to change careers _____

___ 9. Not working to your level of capability _____

___ 10. Termination from job _____

___ 11. Other career or educational consequences: specify

_____

_____

Other Consequences

___ 1. Loss of important friendships _____

_____

___ 2. Loss of interest in hobbies or activities _____

_____

___ 3. Few or no friends because of relationship problems

_____

_____

___ 4. Financial problems _____

_____

___ 5. Illegal activities (arrests or near-arrests) _____

_____

___ 6. Court or legal involvement _____

_____

___ 7. Lawsuits _____

_____

___ 8. Prison or workhouse _____

_____

___ 9. Stealing or embezzling to support behavior _____

_____

___ 10. Other consequences _____

_____

As you think about the consequences you checked as you went through the last few pages, what new insights or thoughts came to you? Please record these in your journal. Record how it feels to know what the costs have been to you.

As you worked through the consequences inventory, you should have noticed a variety of emotions. You certainly should have felt anger, maybe enough anger that you determined to change your patterns. Your anger can fortify you to take the actions you must to care for yourself. It will also empower you to overthrow the old rules of secrecy and betrayal and to be honest about what you see and feel. No more will you disbelieve the obvious and believe the improbable. In the future, your anger will make you intolerant of being exploited and used. Not only will it be okay to upset people, you may even find occasions when you *enjoy* upsetting them.

As you went through the various consequences you experienced, you also probably had feelings of sadness, loss and regret. That means you started accessing the pain stage of your grieving process. Knowing your own hurt and expressing that hurt is critical to healing. First of all, the sadness moves the survivor beyond the anger. Sometimes those in trauma bonds hold on to the anger as a way to stay connected to the abuser. This anger stems from blame and rage and prevents the survivor from experiencing her pain. An example would be the divorcing couple who start off expressing their anger and telling the stories about why they are angry to all their friends. One partner, however, moves beyond that point and realizes that he, too, has significant responsibility for what happened. This partner learns from his experience and goes on to reconstruct his life. He even remarries. The other partner stays stuck in the anger, and nine years later is still telling the blaming stories to anyone who will still listen. That partner has used anger to stay in the relationship, and is probably too scared to accept the pain of the loss.

Let's return to Tom and Barbara's situation. Tom's therapist, Sam, explained to Tom how stuck anger could be a type of *negative intimacy* in a trauma bond. By blaming the other for the problems in his life, the blaming partner can prevent the actual acceptance of the loss of the relationship or the losses caused by the relationship. *Healthy anger* expresses limitations—i.e., what is acceptable and what is not. *Blaming anger* recycles the history of betrayal and all the intense feelings that are part of a trauma bond. It is a negative way to keep the old person around.

Sam gave Tom an assignment to help him. First, he asked Tom to make a list of people Tom had hurt in this process. Further, he wanted Tom to add to that list all those people that Tom and Barbara had hurt together. When Tom was finished, he was stunned to realize that his responsibilities went far beyond just his compulsive relationship patterns. To admit, for example, that he had been compliant in things he did not want to do was not so bad. However, to admit that he also had been vengeful and victimizing to Barbara was extremely difficult to own, even with Sam's help. After all, Barbara was the one with the outrageous behavior. Tom had to admit that he had done dishonorable things as well, and that the craziness he and Barbara created together had hurt many whom he loved deeply. Sam pushed Tom to understand his responsibility so he could understand his own role in his losses. (You may wish to make a list similar to Tom's in your journal. Record what feelings you have about harm you may have caused.)

To finally grieve means to accept that your life did not turn out the way you wanted, the way you deserved or the way it should have. There is an existential reality we all must face that is best captured in the serenity prayer that is the heart of most Twelve-Step programs: *God grant me the serenity to accept the things I cannot change, the courage to change the things I can, and the wisdom to know the difference.* Those who are trauma-bonded have to accept not only the reality of compulsive relationships but also the accumulated losses in their lives going back to whatever created the original working model for relationships.

Viktor Frankl observed that those who survived the concentration camps often had one essential characteristic: They were able to transform suffering into meaning. I believe survivors of any form of abuse have that essential task. Out of the indescribable pain comes clarity of belief and depth of purpose. They become people of substance, with no more tolerance for living in the lie. They know evil for what it is and arm themselves with rituals that keep the meaning close to their hearts. They have a high regard for that which connects, and reject all that divides or hides. Inescapable pain creates enduring honesty and accountability. To take the position that "I am the way I am because of how my family was or because of how they abused me" is to miss the point. You are a participant. As with any addiction, you are powerless, but you have a responsibility to do something about it now. You are responsible for your behavior.

Consider the Greek story of Orestes. Atreus, the grandfather of Orestes, challenged the gods—always a mistake for the Greeks—and as a result his whole family was cursed. Atreus's daughter-in-law, Clytemnestra, murdered her husband, Agamemnon. This act trapped her son, Orestes, between the highest priority of the Greek code of honor, avenging his father's death, and the worst crime of the Greeks, killing his mother. In the end, he murdered his mother. His punishment was to be pursued by the Furies, frightening harpies who tormented him. Orestes was bound to lose either way. He was powerless.

Even though the gods were willing to excuse his solution, Orestes did not duck responsibility. At his trial, he pointed out to all the gods assembled that it was he, no one else, who killed his mother. All he asked for was to be allowed to do something to get the curse lifted. The gods, moved by his integrity, gave him tasks to perform. When Orestes completed those tasks, the Furies were transformed into the Eumenides, the three sources of wisdom. M. Scott Peck wrote about Orestes's nonvictim stance:

Being an inevitable result of the original curse upon the House of Atreus, the Furies also symbolize the fact that mental illness is a family affair, created in one by one's parents and grandparents as the sins of the father are visited upon the children. But Orestes did not blame his family—his parents or his grandfather—as he well might have. Nor did he blame the gods or "fate." Instead he accepted his condition as one of his own making and undertook the effort to heal it. It was a lengthy process, just as most therapy tends to be lengthy. But as a result he was healed, and through this healing process of his own effort, the very things that had once caused him agony became the same things that brought him wisdom.[6]

Like Orestes, survivors cannot afford to blame others. The path of awareness brings them ultimately to acceptance of what their reality is, including their own part, and, like Orestes, they have to take action—which is the focus of our next chapter.

6

WHAT IS THE PATH OF ACTION?

> We must always hold truth, as we can best determine it, to be more important, more vital to our self-interest than our comfort. Conversely, we most always consider our personal discomfort relatively unimportant, and indeed, even welcome it in the service for truth. Mental health is an ongoing process of dedication to reality at all costs.
>
> M. SCOTT PECK, *THE ROAD LESS TRAVELED*

"So, do you want it to be different?" John asked his workshop class. Participants in the week-long workshop on trauma bonding all vigorously nodded their heads. "If you do, you will have to give up compulsive rescuing!" John responded. As John gave examples about rescuing behavior—or, as he described it, "pathological giving"—various participants groaned or laughed in self-recognition. John talked about identifying specific behaviors as "bottom line" behaviors. These are behaviors you refuse to do any more. Instead of repeating these behaviors, you develop other coping strategies that are healthy.

A teacher from northern New York asked, "What is the difference between healthy nurturing or care and coming to the rescue? I would like to think I am a caring person." John responded by pointing out that if you attempt to help a butterfly break out of its cocoon, it may die. The butterfly needs the struggle to be strong. You can be supportive without doing for others what they can do for themselves. As a general rule, it is best to help only when help is truly needed. John added that from a trauma perspective, it is insane to help someone else exploit you. From an addiction perspective, rescuing may only add to the intensity and the insanity of old, addictive cycles of behavior.

To illustrate his point, John asked the participants to list all the payoffs to being a savior or hero. Then he asked them to list the actual costs and liabilities. He pulled the group together and made a common list of participants' payoffs and liabilities. Here are some of the comments on their payoff list:

"I can avoid conflict by rescuing them so they will not be upset with me."

"I want people to appreciate me and my efforts."

"I protect my own childhood wounds by overcompensating so others will not feel disappointed or hurt as I did. I end up blocking reality from them."

"I have a reservoir of resentment that excuses my sexual acting out."

"Feeling obligated keeps my shame intact and powerful because I am overextended and behind all the time."

"Rescuing supports my hero role in the family."

"Turmoil prevents success, which is my life script."

"Overextension by meeting the needs of others creates great martyrdom stories."

"Rescuing creates a one-up position from which I can avoid my feelings and intimacy."

"It is one more way for me to obsess about him."

Some of the comments from the liability list are:

"I lost my freedom and ended up owned by those saved."

"I wanted to prevent him from leaving but my helping became so much it forced him to leave."

"It never works and usually backfires."

"I set myself up to be exploited—and then was upset because I felt taken for granted."

"I lost money I could ill afford."

"Real issues were not addressed and I could keep drinking."

"Keeps me in denial—even when it is dangerous for me."

"Feeling important falsely bolstered my sense of worth. Boy, was I surprised when the truth came out!"

John pushed the group to look at the implications of their work. He asked them to write out specific behaviors to abstain from, strategies needed to avoid those behaviors and guidelines for positive caring behaviors. These activities were part of creating a recovery plan to overcome a pattern of traumatic bonding.

In creating this plan, a central decision must be made that depends upon the recovering person's current life circumstances. One path of action is for people who have been in exploitive relationships and have no reason to be in any further contact with the people who hurt them. Here the goal is not to repeat any of the old compulsive patterns in future relationships.

Another path of action is for those who have been in
exploitive relationships and must have limited contact with
the abusing person. Examples would be when there is involvement in ongoing legal action, when there are children common to both parties or when there are professional duties that
require periodic contact.

Finally, a path exists for both parties in a traumatic bond to
fundamentally reconstruct the relationship in a healthy way.
This will take an extraordinary amount of work, but in some
cases it can be done. Usually these are marital or family relationships, but it can happen in professional settings as well.
All survivors should know all three paths since, more than
likely, they will at some point in their lives need the skills
involved in each.

THE PATH OF NO CONTACT

Sue fell in love with her counselor in treatment. She
declared her love for him in a counseling session and he
admitted that he was both attracted to her and had feelings for
her. At the time she was convinced that their meeting was a
"cosmic" happening. With new doors opening up to her in
sobriety, she felt sure that meeting him at that time was not an
accident but destiny. After she left treatment they were sexual
for several months. She was in ecstasy. She had never met a
man like him—so gentle, kind, handsome and competent.
There were some problems, however. He was married, with
two small children, but his wife was a shrew. Then there was an
intervention and it turned out that he had other relationships—or women who thought they had a relationship with
him. Sue was willing to stand by him through that, but then
he cut off the relationship when she said that he had been
inappropriate.

Sue was furious. In her heart she knew that if they could
have just set aside the professional rules, rules that were so

arbitrary, he would have married her. After all, they did not have sex while she was in treatment; they waited until she left the hospital. Sue believed she had been cheated of the one man with whom she could have been happy.

Sue persisted in this belief. Two different therapists tried to help her understand that she had been exploited. She quit both of them. She then accepted a job offer to move to Baltimore. It was there she met a therapist named Judy. It took almost two years of therapy before Sue fully accepted that what happened to her was exploitive.

One of the first things Judy insisted Sue do was join a Twelve-Step program to continue her recovery on her own addiction. Eventually, she also joined a therapy group of men and women. It was only later that she understood how important those relationships were to help see her through rough times. She discovered the most fundamental rule about trauma bonds: *Trauma bonds can be disrupted when healthy bonds are available.* It was a very powerful night when Sue gave some feedback to one of her group, telling her she was being exploited by the man she had been seeing.

So often in therapy we can see in others the issues we wrestle with ourselves. Her therapist then asked Sue to explain how that felt to the other woman. While explaining, it became clear to Sue how the affair with her counselor was part of a life pattern; she had a history of one "cosmic" relationship after another. Each was characterized by an "impossible situation" and an exploitation of power and intimacy. Sue was also an incest victim, an impossible situation involving the exploitation of power and intimacy. Her support network became the emotional safety net she needed when she could finally admit the truth to herself.

Finding supportive, healthy relationships is the foundation of recovery. Usually this means establishing a relationship with a competent therapist. As with Sue, it often means participating in some form of therapy group. It means also participating in support groups that fit your circumstances. Support is the ground floor of any recovery effort. See the appendix for an extensive listing of support groups and resources for change.

One of the principal functions of a support network is to tell your story to a group of people who will understand what happened to you because it also happened to them. One of the few core strategies proven to help prisoners who have been tortured and sexually molested is the *testimony method.* Torture, especially sexual torture, is designed to break down a prisoner's identity. Political refugees, prisoners, inmates of concentrations camps and slaves have endured this process throughout history and down to the present day. People who specialize in helping these survivors with their trauma have found in recent years that the first part of recovery is to give a detailed description of what happened to a sympathetic audience. For this testimony to work it must go through a *reframing.* This reframing puts an individual story in a larger context, enabling other prisoners or captives to see their own story as part of a greater struggle.[1] By telling their story, they are "reunited" with other humans who care for them. It now means something to survive. That sense of survival begins a process of restoration to the human community. Healthy bonding can now occur.

Alcoholics Anonymous started on that principle. Carl Jung had written Bill W. and told him that change would probably not occur if alcoholics did not pass on their story. This principle has proved effective in an almost uncountable number of contexts and has shaped our culture in a significant way. Whether you are an incest survivor, a domestic abuse victim or a victim of clergy sexual misconduct, there is a place to tell your story, receive support and make meaning out of your experience.

The other contribution support networks can make concerns boundary development. Supportive people in the survivor's life can help the survivor draw a line in the sand that says: "I will not tolerate this any more in my life." With that limit set, the survivor begins reclaiming herself.

Boundary development is critical for those who grow up unable to tell if abuse is present or not. *Figuring out what you do not want forces you to determine what you do want.* That means you have to know who you are and then value yourself enough to mean what you say. An old Buddhist saying suggests that to say "no" means you have to know what "yes" is. That process forms a sense of self—which is precisely what was lost in the trauma bond.

In Sue's case, and on her therapist's advice, she stopped dating altogether for a period of time. She needed time out from the roller coaster of instant and "cosmic" relationships. Understanding the cycle she was in and the role of victimization she played was transformative in her life. When she started dating again, she worked very hard to keep her boundaries: the types of men she saw, when and under what circumstances she saw them and what she expected of them. Were they honorable men or "impossible situations"? At times she missed the intensity, but for the most part she was amazed at how much easier things were for her.

For trauma bonds to be disrupted, the survivor must be able to identify the cycles of abuse and the roles of victim, victimizer and rescuer. This is how the relationship system and the roles of the survivor in that system can change. This will create a compassion for the self in much the way you may have experienced it when writing your story in the third person earlier in this book (see chapter 5). That exercise created a "psychological distance" so that you could see yourself. This is similar to the way Sue could see the problem in another woman in her group easier than in herself. When Sue's perception shifted, she had a better sense of what it meant to "care *for* herself" and to take "care *of* herself."

Most therapists are trained to help the identification process with the use of metaphor. Metaphors become part of the story.

Like medicine men and medicine women of earlier times, healers can sometimes help people on the journey more through a story or symbol that represents what needs to be done.[2] An extremely helpful example of a healing metaphor used within a trauma context is the concept of *remodeling*. When remodeling a home, you restructure it so it is more functional, move livable and more attractive. You work also to preserve those parts that have special character and meaning. Therapist Rochelle Scheela has broken the remodeling metaphor down into six specific areas:[3]

> falling apart: final acceptance that the home can no longer be sustained the way it is and that it has to be remodeled
>
> taking on the remodeling: decision to personally do the work because the task is now unavoidable
>
> tearing out: assessing the damage, understanding the original design and sorting out what is salvageable
>
> rebuilding: replacing damaged parts and adding new, more functional parts, but making them part of a seamless, attractive design
>
> doing the upkeep: maintaining the whole home so it does not return to disrepair
>
> moving on: decision to move on to more remodeling projects

Anyone who has remodeled knows that these steps seldom happen in an orderly fashion. A survivor may be rebuilding one area and tearing down another. Also, life is unpredictable enough that some more falling apart might occur.

For Sue, the actual remodeling took almost five years. In looking back, she wrote off the first two years as being in denial. To put it in remodeling language, she did not take on the task even though people around her were willing to help. At the end, however, she could hardly believe how different her life was. She was productive, focused and in a happy relationship. She now joked about the days of "impossible situations" and "cosmic relationships." Getting to that point involved both tearing down and rebuilding. On the tearing down side, Sue had to abandon relationship rules that went back to childhood. Judy, her therapist, helped her with strategies for desensitizing around some of her original trauma with her father. Therapists today have access to technology, such as *eye movement desensitization,* which can help lower reactivity time. For Sue, the result was that she no longer had to manage her feelings by creating the exhilaration of "cosmic" connections.

Judy also insisted that Sue create a recovery plan. Similar to what participants did in the workshop described at the beginning of the chapter, Sue had to be very specific about relationship behaviors in which she would and would not engage. A recovery plan consists of three parts. *First, you must identify bottom-line behaviors.* These are the behaviors you simply do not do. For Sue, a bottom-line behavior was not to date anyone who had authority over her. *Second, you must create a boundaries list.* These are limits to be observed around activities and relationships that would put you at risk or that do not add to your recovery. For Sue, this meant that she agreed not to be sexual with anyone with whom she did not have a relationship for at least six months. If she decided she wanted to be sexual, she would talk to her therapy group before taking action. Sue understood that this was not punitive, but rather a way for her to lower potential intensity and preserve her perspective. *Finally, a recovery plan asks what kind of behavior you want in a relationship.* How will you know if a relationship is successful? One of Sue's criteria was "waking up each day feeling unafraid and happy."

At the conclusion of this chapter, there is a model recovery plan. Before exploring that, however, there are two other paths that need to be understood. First, the path of limited contact. Second, the path of full relationship.

THE PATH OF LIMITED CONTACT

Sometimes there is no escaping contact. Children can be involved. There is a court process to complete. Both parties work in the same profession in the same city. You own property or businesses together. Finances have to be settled. Something will exist that requires you to see the person who has been problematic for you. The path of limited contact may be your only option.

Such was the case with Catherine who left her husband, Fred, after thirteen years of marriage. They had three children together, ages thirteen, eleven and three. Catherine was Fred's second wife. Fred was an attorney and Catherine had been his secretary. They had an affair while Fred was still married. Catherine got pregnant and Fred left his first wife with whom he had two children.

There were warning signs for Catherine. She will always remember the night Fred's ex-wife dropped off the kids, looked at Catherine and said, "You are in a world of trouble." When Catherine asked what she meant, the woman actually looked at her with some compassion and said, "I was his first secretary," and walked out the door.

There were many scary things about Fred. He was one of the best litigators around. He was known for ruthlessly defending his clients and liked being a "hired gun." He was incredibly smart and could anticipate his opponents' moves. He was a large man, over six-foot-four, and prone to raging. He felt his outbursts were okay, he would joke, as long as he did not "leave any marks." He was rough with sex and loved bondage scenes. He was intimidating, ruthless, handsome, smooth and, as Catherine was to learn, totally without scruples.

The early years of the marriage were hectic. Two children

right away kept Catherine very busy. As the years went on, Fred's drinking increased and there was episodic violence. It became clear that sex and violence were fused for Fred. Their youngest child was actually a product of Fred's rape of Catherine. If that were not enough, during that second pregnancy Catherine discovered the following in the space of one week: Fred was using prostitutes for sadomasochistic sex; he had been involved with her very own sister; and he had been guilty of jury tampering and witness bribery for a client with underworld connections. She resolved to leave.

The nightmare of leaving made the marriage look like a holiday. She suddenly became Fred's "opponent." She faced a legal barrage. Every day there was another legal maneuver. Depositions, accusations and motions became a way of life. There was conflict over custody. Arrogant, punitive faxes about problems he had with her parenting were routine. He had her own family almost convinced that she had an emotional problem. When he urged treatment, she started making up lies about him. That actually worked until her sister collapsed under the strain and owned up to her affair with him. Since Catherine was the "hero" in a family that had problems of alcoholism and violence, issues became layered upon issues. Her abusive father was absolutely on Fred's side until Catherine's sister came forward with her affair. There was one more ingredient: Fred's firm was representing Catherine's father's company in an extremely convoluted court case that, if it failed, would leave her parents impoverished at retirement.

Catherine felt like she was in a battle zone. The worst part was that Fred was good at not "leaving any marks," so she could not get court protection or prove anything. During the whole settlement period, she had to see Fred in court and had to deal with the children seeing Fred. Being in a group and having a therapist was lifesaving for Catherine. Her therapist explained how in trauma bonding the roles are so strong, you have to have help from people who care about you and who know the real situation. They can help debrief or *de-role* the victim from the intensity of the bond. She used the concept of *bookending*. For example, before a deposition she had to meet with two members of her group and have a therapy appointment scheduled immediately after. Catherine learned never to have scheduled contact with Fred without first getting a stress inoculation of support. She would literally get coaching from people in her network about what to expect and how to handle it. She also never talked to Fred without immediately calling someone to de-role.

With her therapist's and attorney's help, she established limits with Fred. These boundaries improved things, but Fred was very skillful at breaching those boundaries by creating ambushes. Catherine had to learn what many victims have found out: Boundaries are great when you can plan things out, but often you will need strategies to use "in the moment." This is where Catherine learned about the *stillness*. This exercise is based on a story about the Royal Navy. Sailors are instructed that whenever they hear a specific whistle it means something has happened so serious that everyone on the ship is in immediate danger. When that whistle blows, the sailors stop what they are doing, since they have only moments, look at what resources are around them, and do the right thing. It is called the *stillness*. For Catherine, this meant that when Fred created a situation that demanded an immediate response from her and tried to stampede her into a decision she might later regret, she had a right to the stillness. She would stop, center herself, and see what her options were before responding. She learned to tell Fred that she needed ten minutes to respond, ten minutes that would give her time to think or make a phone call. The metaphor of the stillness was a gift to Catherine. She grew to appreciate a window of time, even if only seconds, so she could do the right thing.

At her therapist's recommendation, Catherine went to a residential facility for an intensive workshop intended for abuse survivors who struggled with addictive issues. It was a gift in many ways. For the first time it became clear to her how her working model for relationships was in part responsible for her involvement with Fred. Catherine started to make all kinds of connections about what happened in her original family and in her life with Fred. For example, it was no surprise that her father chose Fred's firm for his company. They had similar values and ways of operating.

In the workshop she also learned about the concept of *carried shame*. This means that the victim feels shameful and the perpetrator shameless.[4] Victims are set up in the exploitive system to devalue themselves as a defense against examining what the abuser is doing. They feel at fault because they are told they are responsible for whatever problems there are. As long as they feel at fault, the abuser is in the "one-up" position.

Catherine learned a wonderful metaphor to help with the shame issue. Her instructor compared having boundaries to having a zipper.[5] Most people can control their zippers from the inside. If someone asks them for information they do not want to give, they simply do not give it. If asked to do something that feels uncomfortable, they say no. If told they are bad or responsible for something they did not do, they figure those comments are really about the other person, not them. People who have been tyrannized by terror and invaded often have the zippers on the outside. Anyone can access them. They simply unzip. Victims can be asked information they do not wish to reveal, and they reveal it. They commit to things they do not want to do. They feel responsible when they have done nothing. They can easily be invaded sexually, physically and emotionally. The challenge for the victim is to get the zipper firmly back inside. This requires more than knowing when someone is being abusive. It means being able to say no without shame.

After the workshop, Catherine discovered how helpful it was to be away from all the stress so she could focus on the issues. Her therapist observed that the core to recovery was the ability to psychologically distance from the intensity. Catherine would not always be able to get away, so she needed to develop strategies to help her de-escalate the intensity on a daily basis. Her therapist now taught her the concept of *doing business.* She asked Catherine what she would do if she ordered an item that had to be picked up later. Catherine said she would call, find out when it would be ready, and then pick it up. Her therapist then asked if this would be an emotional event. Catherine, seeing where this was heading, laughed and said no. Her therapist then asked what would happen if she needed to know when the kids would be ready to be picked up from Fred's house. Catherine got the point and responded, "It's an international incident." Then her therapist invited Catherine to role-play such a call with Catherine being Fred and the therapist playing Catherine. It went like this:

> *Catherine: What time will the children be ready?*
> *Fred: So we are going to try to be grown up enough to be on time!*
> *Catherine: All I need to know is what time they will be ready.*
> *Fred: As if you really cared about them.*
> *Catherine: I need the time, Fred.*
> *Fred: What are you going to do about the interrogatories I sent you?*
> *Catherine: My attorney will respond to that. What time will the children be ready?*
> *Fred: Three o'clock.*
> *Catherine: Three o'clock. Thank you.*

All Catherine needed was the time. The rest was all intensity. Fred was expert at provoking responses. Catherine learned she could be expert at focusing on the "business" at hand. Or as she said to the therapist, "getting my zipper turned around."

Changing the abusive system requires a reframing of the interactions in the system. A therapist will ask a victim to revisit a specific scene of abuse. As the victim talks, the therapist becomes a coach, helping the victim understand the reactions that occur. The therapist then teaches the client how to manage her feelings more effectively. Clinicians call this *cognitive restructuring*, which means the victim creates a new map or working model for the relationship. Reframing is one of the strategies most often used. Reframing means you create a new way of looking at the interaction. For example: "When your father says those sarcastic statements and says he is only joking, he is wrong. He is being cruel and mean-spirited. He is trying to connect with you but doing it in a horrible way." Another example for Catherine was the conception of her third child. Her therapist insisted that Catherine start referring to the event as a sexual assault. The shift within Catherine with that reframe was astounding because she knew it was true.

Catherine's recovery plan included bottom-line behaviors for both Fred and her father. With Fred she would no longer share any emotions or friendly talk with him. They were designed to drag her back into the system. With her father she would no longer tolerate his sarcastic remarks, even by ignoring them. As one of her boundaries, Catherine decided to have her attorney address Fred on anything legal or financial. She personally would no longer respond. Among her relationship goals, Catherine put down that she would know she was in a good relationship when she could fully be herself. She felt she had lived in fear for so long that she had forgotten what it was like to be with people without being on guard.

FULL RELATIONSHIP

For many, the restoration of exploitive relationships would be impossible or pointless. If the clergyman who abused you was now in prison it would be difficult, insane and futile to seek him out for spiritual care. But what if it is your father who is in prison for sexual abuse of his children? Or what if it is your husband, with whom you've had five children, who is making extraordinary efforts to change his life? What criteria would you use? Here are some suggestions. First, if addictions are involved, they must be addressed. That means the abuser must willingly go to treatment and commit to a program of recovery. Second, the victim must be in therapy and in a support program for recovery. All members of the support network must be informed as to what is happening. Third, there must be a period of separation so that the victim can experience living independent of the abuser and can observe how the abuser lives when the two are separated. If those conditions are met, add these criteria:

  a clear track record of non-abusing behavior

  a verifiable commitment to therapy and Twelve-Step group attendance

  a coordinated effort of joint therapy involving both partners

  an acceptance by the abuser of the consequences of his actions

  a clear and earnest effort to make amends to all who have been hurt

  an agreement for zero tolerance of old behavior

Let's use the circle analogy once again. Can both parties remain in the circle of intimacy at the same time? For the victim, how does it feel to be in the other's presence?

There is an old Al-anon piece of wisdom that says "nothing major the first year." That means that after a year of recovery, things will look extremely different. Doing anything that is not reversible may be premature. Also, the victim has much to do to work on his or her own healing. Once that foundation is there, a new relationship might be negotiated. Remember, the principal problem trauma victims have is reactivity. During the initial phases of recovery, monitoring your reactivity to others is very important. The focus should remain on you, not the abuser.

Consider the story of Marge. She was married to a Protestant minister named Brad who served as pastor to 8,000 people in the wealthiest suburb in the city. He worked upwards of ninety or more hours a week. When the tension was high he would, on occasion, rage at Marge and the kids. Sometimes he was extremely punitive with the children, exacting consequences that far outweighed whatever the child had done. Sometimes in his anger he struck Marge, which she found shattering. Then he would make up to her and rationalize his angry outbreaks as a result of working too hard and trying to serve the Lord. She was proud of his work but she also was lonely raising their children. And as time went on, she was progressively more scared. As a minister's wife, she knew that to get help in their denomination might mean the end of Brad's career. What would they do then? So she kept quiet, hiding behind the veneer of "everything is good in the minister's family."

The veneer fell off, however, when a friend called Marge and asked to meet with her. When they got together, the friend brought a woman who was called an advocate. The advocate worked in the bishop's office. They came to tell her that Brad had been having an affair with a parishioner. Brad had attempted to cut it off and the parishioner had gone to the bishop. Word spread quickly. Seven more women had come forward to the bishop. There was to be an intervention the next day. Before the intervention, they wanted to know if she knew about these women, how things were with her, and whether she would help them. Marge was stunned. She felt like a fool. On the other hand, this was the first time she felt she could tell anyone what life with Brad was like. She started sobbing as she told them about her pain.

Brad was admitted to an inpatient treatment facility for his sex addiction and cocaine abuse. Marge and the kids attended family week. They found out that Brad had a whole life none of them knew or could even guess at. To begin with, they had no idea about his cocaine use or that he took loose money donated on Sundays to support his drug habit. It was how he got himself through. His secret life was a fast life, a life enabled by wealthy parishioners, especially women.

Raised in a rigid farm family, Brad had been steadily and severely abused, both physically and sexually, since the age of five. The perpetrators of the abuse were farm hands. He had also experienced work abuse, working at least twelve hours a day every day he was not in school. Overwork and violence had long been part of his life.

After doing a family genogram in family week, everybody could see how the problems for both Marge and Brad went back for generations. Marge and the kids went to therapy when they returned from family week. Marge's therapist asked her to put a moratorium on deciding whether to divorce Brad or not. He had been sent by the church to an extended care facility. He remained there for eight months. When he returned, he found an apartment of his own. Marge was struck by how there was no pressure from Brad to move back in. It also became clear to her that he was committed to working on their relationship.

In fact, there was a lot about Brad that was different. He was patient and open with the kids. In family therapy he shared several stories in which he cried deeply in their presence. He clearly felt shame and remorse for what he had done. Marge was struck about how being with him now was like what it used to be when they were first together.

Brad also began taking the initiative in their relationship. He asked Marge to go a Twelve-Step couples retreat. Out of that retreat they joined a Recovering Couples Anonymous group, or RCA. It was in RCA that Marge felt real healing begin for her and Brad. They met many couples who had been through similar dramas and who were committed to supportive relationships. They used the metaphor of the three-legged stool. The three legs represented "my recovery," "your recovery" and "our recovery as a couple."

On the retreat, the lead couple described relationships as a "blending of epics." Each couple had the task of blending families whose traditions and rules spanned many generations. If a family history was filled with trauma, addiction and violence, it was virtually impossible not to repeat the sins of the previous generation. When the inevitable relationship crisis came, there was always the option to move on to another person. Yet if that were done, the process of blending would have to begin all over again. Better to face the issues with the person you are with, then see if the relationship works.

RCA couples were no strangers to the problem of intensity. One of the first things Brad and Marge had to do was to write a "fair fight" contract. If you care about someone, over time you will have conflict with them. But many couples never firmly establish how they will settle their issues. For Marge and Brad the impact was revolutionary. One of their rules was "no dramatic exits," which Brad would do often and Marge dreaded. Once he agreed to that, it freed her up to be honest with her issues. As a couple they learned that, as trauma survivors, they needed to contain their reactivity. And the fair fight contract helped them immensely.

Another RCA concept that was helpful was *couple shame.* Individuals have shame, and so do couples. Marge and Brad had a lot of shame about the public outcry over Brad's behavior. They were also profoundly embarrassed with their children about the chaos of their life. They recognized that both of them contributed to the problem, and that they could get into deep despair about it. Fortunately, they had a wonderful sponsor couple who helped them not be so hard on themselves. When Brad and Marge felt despairing, or without hope, they called their sponsor couple.

Conjoint couples therapy was also extremely helpful. They learned about intimacy and got help for when they had trouble negotiating the new rules for making decisions. The biggest lesson of all, however, was about blame. One of their therapists talked about the "no fault" system.They learned it was more important to find out how the problem happened than it was to blame each other for the problem. It was extraordinary progress when they could sit down and pinpoint the process that brought them to crisis and not be defensive or accusing. In fact, a relationship goal for each of them was to take responsibility for whatever they did that made things harder for the other.

They also negotiated boundaries. Marge did not want to talk about serious matters after nine o'clock at night. She was too tired by that time and it was always counterproductive. Another bottom-line behavior for Marge was not to protect Brad from the consequences of his behavior. She learned to stay out of the way completely.

Brad and Marge had a number of tough years. Brad could not work as a minister and money was extremely tight. Marge went back to school to study theology, which was very demanding. But they worked on their therapy and remained very active in their own recovery groups as well as RCA. Their children matured, went to college and started families of their own.

Eleven years after the intervention on Brad, he was accepted back into active ministry. Marge finished theology school and was ordained into the ministry as well. For her, it was the realization of a forbidden dream. (Marrying Brad was as close to the ministry as she ever thought she'd get.) She and Brad began serving as assistant co-pastors of a small church in Northern California.

It was a powerful Sunday when the new co-pastors told their story. The people loved them, as did their children.

THE DIMENSIONS OF RECOVERY

Whichever path is yours—no contact, limited contact or full relationship—key dimensions of recovery must be addressed. They are:

> healthy bonds—must be available in the form of therapy and support groups
>
> boundary development—critical to restoring the ability of the victim to take care of self
>
> role development—allows new interaction beyond victim and victimizer
>
> trauma resolution—diminishes the power of the original events and makes reactivity less of a problem
>
> systems change—necessary to move into non-exploitive relationships
>
> sense of self—the essential developmental process that has been disrupted and needs to be restored
>
> key metaphors—critical for helping to develop a new "working model"
>
> recovery plan—makes concrete the recovery changes

Figure 6.1 summarizes all eight dimensions of recovery in each of the specific paths. It is important to notice the activities in each path because, more than likely, you may eventually need to use some of the strategies from all the paths as you move toward recovery. For example, you might be in "no contact" now but run into someone you need to "limit contact" with in the future.

Figure 6.1. Trauma Bond Recovery Paths

RECOVERY DIMENSION	NO CONTACT	LIMITED CONTACT	FULL RELATIONSHIP
1. Healthy Bonds	Establish support network to tell the story	Group or community can debrief or de-role victim	Group or community supports relationship
2. Boundary Development	Learn boundary-setting strategies	Strategies for using boundaries in the moment	Negotiate new partnership/ relationship
3. Role Development	Identify roles of victim, victimizer, rescuer	Develop new working model for relationships	Identify relationship patterns of healthy intimacy
4. Trauma Resolution	Trauma desensitization	Psychological distance from intensity	Develop fair fight contract
5. Systems Change	Identify cycles of abuse	Reframe traumatic interactions	No fault system
6. Sense of self	Work for self-acceptance and self-care	Strategies for resisting carried shame	Strategies for resisting couple shame
7. Key Metaphors	Remodeling; write a story	Stillness; doing business; bookending	Three-legged stool; the blending of epics
8. Recovery Plan	Three recovery areas for no contact	Three recovery areas for limited contact	Three recovery areas for full relationship

Before going on to the next chapter, please complete your recovery plan carefully. Bring it to your therapist or support group and ask for feedback. It is important to complete this work before starting the activities of the next chapter.

RECOVERY PLAN FOR COMPULSIVE RELATIONSHIPS

Step One: *Finish the Story:* Return to chapter 5 and the assignment "Write the Story." In that assignment you were asked to write your story using third-person pronouns, and to write it as if it were a fairy tale: "Once there was a little girl . . ." is how you started. Now finish your work by adding a page or two describing how you would like to see the story end. When complete, take it to your support group and therapist and read it out loud. Record your experiences in your journal.

Step Two: *Establish Level of Contact:* List below those people who have been abusive in your life and who are on no contact, limited contact or full relationship levels of contact. Remember, there is no right or wrong list—only what serves as the best match for you.

No Contact	Limited Contact	Full Relationship
1. _____	1. _____	1. _____
2. _____	2. _____	2. _____
3. _____	3. _____	3. _____
4. _____	4. _____	4. _____
5. _____	5. _____	5. _____

Step Three: *Bottom-Line Behaviors:* These are destructive behaviors from which you wish to abstain. Write very concrete descriptions of what you do not want to do.

Example: Sue

   A. Date no one who has any authority or power over me.

1._____

2._____

3._____

4._____

5._____

6._____

7._____

8._____

9._____

10._____

Step Four: *Boundaries List:* These are behaviors to avoid because they put you at risk or they do not add to your recovery. Check them by seeing what "exceptions" you can find and rewrite accordingly.

Example: Catherine

   A. I will not discuss legal or financial matters with Fred. He must always go through my attorney.

1._____

2._____

3._____

4._____

5._____

6._____

7._____

8._____

9._____

10._____

Step Five: *Relationship Goals:* These are behaviors that would constitute relationship health for you. Again, make the statements as concrete as possible.

Example: Marge

   A. I will take responsibility and own explicitly behavior that has been harmful to my partner.

1._____

2._____

3._____

4._____

5._____

6._____

7._____

8._____

9._____

10._____

7

FURTHER STEPS ON THE PATH TO RECOVERY

This consistent pattern of hyperarousal alternating with numbing has been noticed following such a vast array of different traumas, such as combat, rape, kidnapping, spouse abuse, natural disasters, accidents, concentration camp experiences, incest, and child abuse.

BESSEL VAN DER KOLK[1]

Sitting in my office, Traci described her nightmare step by step. It was her last week of treatment before returning home. She was scared. She was a strong woman, pretty, in her early forties, with four children. Two years previously she had started an affair with her psychologist, a woman named Sandi. The psychologist had twenty years of experience in her field. She also was a highly respected teacher at a nearby university. Traci was very attracted to Sandi's charisma, intelligence and wit. She continued in therapy while they were dating. Finally Sandi said that they needed to stop therapy because it was unprofessional. Then she suggested that they could move in together. Traci left her husband of fifteen years so she could be free to be involved with the therapist.

Sandi took over Traci's life, controlling everything from job to children. When Traci tried to break it off and moved to an apartment of her own, Sandi battered her front door down. Sandi also made direct threats on the lives of Traci's husband and children. The list of abuses over the two-year period seemed endless. I asked Traci what her reaction would be if Sandi busted through her front door again. With a tear rolling down her cheek she admitted, "To tell the truth, I can't wait to see her again."

Traci actually was on schedule. She was very clear about the nature of the abuses, the life consequences it caused, her own personal issues that were part of it and the family dynamics with her husband and children. She had made much progress. So she was mystified as to why she still had these feelings for someone who had hurt her and her loved ones so badly. I told her that the feelings are normal. In the language of addictions we call them cravings; they do not go away simply because you understand. Many get to the point of understanding but get pulled back in by the emotional reactivity. The key is to dismantle the reactivity and the other trauma solutions that support traumatic bonding. The relapse prevention plan you just completed focuses specifically on the relationship life itself. Now we need to focus on how reactivity, arousal, blocking, splitting, deprivation, shame and repetition are used in that relationship. Only then will you have sufficient distance to recognize that the feelings are not about reality. They are like the Sirens of the ancient Greeks who seduced unwary sailors off course, where they crashed on the rocks hidden under the sea.

This chapter is organized around a series of exercises to help you with the emotional distance you need. Doing these exercises well will require much work and time. Groups who have used these activities will often spend up to two or three weeks on a single section. Take your time. There are rewards for doing these exercises thoroughly. The first is that a thorough relapse plan will, the more you work it, become a process of self-definition. Second, the plan will increase your self-knowledge and give you new skills to cope with stress and trauma. You will be tempted to skip to the next chapter and not return to these activities. If you do, you will experience what Traci and others have found: that it is not sufficient to simply understand. You will need skills to cope. You will also need your support group, journal and therapist to make the most out of what is asked of you. Some of you might say that your life was relatively problem-free until you got into the specific relationship that prompted you to read this book. For some people that will be true, but all it takes is one trauma bond to bring terror to your life. Do the exercises anyway.

Traci returned home and started going to a therapist who worked hard with her on the activities you are about to do. Traci reported Sandi to the state board and has achieved a working relationship with her husband in which there is good co-parenting. She wrote me about her progress and then mentioned she had recently read the novel by Mario Puzo called *The Last Don*. In the novel, there is a woman whose husband and family were murdered in front of her on her wedding night as retaliation for a gangland slaying. She stayed loyal to the family and even cooked for the father (the Don), until finally she went insane.[2] Traci's comment about this character was, "I did more than understand the plight of Rose Marie. I know what happened to her." Traci was telling me that understanding was not enough. The knowledge has to get to the core of who you are if you are to survive.

Two suggestions before you proceed. First, review your self-assessment scores from chapter 2. Now that you are more clear about the problem, your assessment may shift. Second, if you get stuck, review the appropriate sections in the first two chapters to help you think about a specific trauma solution. Now to begin.

REACTIVITY RECOVERY PLAN

Survivors of terror tend to react in extremes. Their "alarm system" is set to hypersensitive. The result is inner turmoil, personal chaos and relationship dysfunction. The other trauma solutions are an effort to manage this reactivity. By finding healthy ways to manage the internal reactions, you will be less vulnerable to those dysfunctional coping strategies.

Start by listing ways that you underreact and ways you overreact in the relationships you are concerned about. Give a description of what the reaction is, what the feeling is and the behavior that results from it. Describe a specific event in which that happened. Then describe an appropriate response strategy and what probably would have happened had you done that.

Underreactions

Example: Fear of telling Mother the truth about how I do not like her hitting the children. I keep quiet and my anger comes out at the children. Like when she slapped Jason last week.

Balanced response: I have to tell her clearly what my rules are and that I do not hit my children. If she hits them again, I will limit her contact with them. As long as I am with her, she will respect that and I will have to ignore her comments. She might be open to talking about it. I will tell her how her hitting me has affected me. That might have a real impact.

Overreactions

Example: I get angry at Bill and feel hopeless about ever getting his attention. I love taking his car and doing something destructive to it. Last week I drove his car right through the garage door.

Balanced response: No more dramatic exits. No abuse of his car. I could tell him that I am angry and that we need to talk this through. If he is unwilling, I will take that as a sign as to how badly he wants us to be together. I will use the fair fight contract. Had I used the contract, Bill probably would have listened and I would not have looked like such a fool.

1. Underreaction:

Balanced Response:

2. Underreaction:

Balanced Response:

3. Underreaction:

Balanced Response:

4. Underreaction:

Balanced Response:

5. Underreaction:

Balanced Response:

6. Overreaction:

Balanced Response:

7. Overreaction:

Balanced Response:

8. Overreaction:

Balanced Response:

9. Overreaction:

Balanced Response:

10. Overreaction:

Balanced Response:

Record your reactions in your journal and share with your group.

AROUSAL RECOVERY PLAN

High arousal and intensity bring relief to painful feelings. Absorption in pleasure and high risk dilutes the hurt and pain.

This part of your recovery examines the role of high arousal in the relationship or relationships you are concerned about. First you need to notice what "arousal" addictions you use as part of this relationship.

If you have questions about this exercise reread chapter 1.

Arousal Addictions

1. Sexual behavior (including sadomasochism, swinging, pornography and public sex)

   _____

   _____

2. Drugs (including cocaine, crystal, crack and amphetamines)

   _____

   _____

3. Caffeine, tobacco

   _____

   _____

4. High-risk behaviors

   _____

   _____

5. Gambling (including risky commodities trading and other financial trades or risks)

   _____

   _____

Now you need to look at the intensity of the relationship. In what ways does the relationship create emotional intensity?

Chaos? Fear? Inconsistency? Roller coaster career? High stakes and high risk? Threats? Make a list of the sources of intensity and include an example for each.

Sources of Intensity:

1._____

2._____

3._____

4._____

5._____

Write a plan of action for distancing from the intensity. Plans will vary by the level of contact you intend to have and the sources of intensity. Be very specific about the steps you will take.

Record your reactions in your journal and share with your group.

BLOCKING RECOVERY PLAN

Survivors of abuse seek soothing. Anything to calm, medicate or anesthetize anxiety can be used to block awareness and pain.

This part of your recovery plan examines the role of blocking strategies in the relationship or relationships you are concerned about. First you need to notice what satiation addictions are part of this relationship.

If you have questions about this exercise reread chapter 1.

Satiation Addictions

1. Alcoholism

_____

_____

2. Compulsive eating

_____

_____

3. Compulsive working

_____

_____

4. Depressant drugs

_____

_____

5. Compulsive sex (sex as a way to calm down or go to sleep)

_____

_____

6. Compulsive spending (buying things to feel better)

_____

_____

Soothing Strategies:

1. _____

2. _____

3. _____

4. _____

5. _____

Write a plan for calming yourself in healthy ways. Be very specific about the steps you will take. For example: "Each weekday morning I will meditate for twenty minutes."

Record your reactions in your journal and share with your group.

SPLITTING RECOVERY PLAN

Survivors will split off from reality as a way to deal with their terror and pain. Dissociation (living in an unreal world) then becomes a coping strategy.

This part of your recovery plan examines the role of living in an unreal world in the relationship or relationships you are concerned about. There are many ways to create unreality. Addicts will use obsession and preoccupation as a vehicle to literally be in a trance. First you need to notice if addictive preoccupation was part of this relationship.

Preoccupation and Obsession Used to Escape Reality

Example: obsessing about next sexual episode with abusive partner.

With drugs and alcohol

_____

_____

With sexual behavior

_____

_____

With food

_____

_____

With risk

_____

_____

With perpetrator's addictions (codependency)

_____

_____

With work

_____

_____

Have you used the following as a way to enter another "reality" and avoid what is happening around you and in the relationship?

Hallucinogenic drugs such as LSD and marijuana

_____

_____

Excessive religious or spiritual practice

_____

_____

Immersion in art and music

_____

_____

Compulsive book reading (as in romance or adventure novels)

_____

_____

Compulsive video and TV watching

_____

_____

Living in daydreams

_____

_____

Rehearsing conversations in your head that you never seem to have

_____

_____

Having separate "parts" of yourself you do not let others know about

_____

_____

In trauma bonds, the relationship itself is an escape from reality. Victims will ignore friends, family, work and values to be in a relationship built on deception.

The following diagram is an extremely helpful way to see how such a relationship "splits" reality. You will notice two columns, one for illusion and one for reality. Using the diagram, review the relationship or relationships you are concerned about in light of what you now know about seduction and betrayal. You will see how trauma bonding generated a life based on illusion.

ILLUSION vs. REALITY

ILLUSION	REALITY
First contact: The promise the victimizer made was in the form of a story, or kindness, or compassion for you, or a noble cause. What was that promise? _____ _____ _____	Your vulnerability: You had developmental or unmet needs, or unfinished business that made you vulnerable to the promise for which you would give up all. What was that vulnerability? _____ _____

ILLUSION	REALITY
Validation: The victimizer validated the promise in some way so that you believed things are actually the way they were presented. How was your confidence gained?	
_____ _____ _____	First betrayal: The real intention becomes clear in early abuse or exploitation. What really happened?
Reseduction: The victimizer adds an explanation to the story so that the abuse is understandable. How did the victimizer revalidate the promise so you would stay?	_____ _____ _____
_____ _____ _____	More betrayal: The abuse and exploitation continue in a number of forms. What are the costs to you now because you have stayed?
Reframing: The victimizer interpreted costs to you as minimal and reframed them as necessary for the good of the relationship. What did the victimizer tell you to do about your losses?	_____ _____ _____
_____ _____ _____	Life crisis: Ultimately, reality asserts itself and you realize you can go no further. What loss was significant enough to make you face reality?
	_____ _____ _____

Find a different color pen than the one you used to finish this last section. Go back over the exercise and write in the empty spaces how you could have handled the relationship differently. After completing your comments, look at the other parts of this section, and compose a brief statement of "Ten Rules to Stay in Reality." Record your thoughts in your journal and read your "rules" to your group and therapist.

TEN RULES TO STAY IN REALITY

1. _____
_____
_____

2. _____
_____
_____

3. _____
_____
_____

4. _____
_____
_____

5. _____
_____
_____

6. _____
_____
_____

7. _____
_____

8. _____

_____

_____

9. _____

_____

_____

10. _____

_____

_____

DEPRIVATION RECOVERY PLAN

"What are you doing to take care of yourself?" is one of the most often asked questions in recovery. Self-neglect is one of the common causes of relapse, and it is true that children whose parents neglected them have difficulty taking good care of themselves.

This part of your recovery plan looks at those areas of your life that have gone beyond neglect of yourself and become compulsive deprivation or even compulsive self-harm. First you need to identify forms of compulsive deprivation or self-harm that existed in the relationship(s) that you worry about.

Compulsive Deprivation and Self-Harm

1. Anorexia (self-starvation with food)

   _____

   _____

2. Sexual anorexia (aversion to sex)

   _____

   _____

3. Compulsive saving or hoarding

   _____

   _____

4. Compulsive cleaning

_____

_____

5. Cutting or hurting self

_____

_____

6. Hair pulling or skin picking

_____

_____

7. Body piercing or excessive tattoos

_____

_____

8. Compulsive exercising (excessive athleticism)

_____

_____

9. Compulsive debting (so much debt you cannot care for yourself) or compulsive saving

_____

_____

10. Compulsive working (working to the point of exhaustion and numbness)

_____

_____

Relationship Deprivation

Were you ever:

1. Asked to sacrifice in extreme ways?

_____

_____

2. Asked to endure extreme hardship?

_____

_____

3. Denied medical care?

_____

_____

4. Asked to work extreme hours?

_____

_____

5. Denied clothing?

_____

_____

6. Asked to deplete your own funds for the relationship?

_____

_____

7. Asked to give up significant friendships?

_____

_____

8. Asked to give up important family relationships?

_____

_____

9. Forced to live in inhospitable conditions?

_____

_____

10. Asked to give up a job or make self-destructive career decisions?

_____

_____

Review the above and make a list of what a healthy, caring human being would do for herself.

1._____

2._____

3._____

4._____

5._____

6._____

7._____

8._____

9._____

10._____

11._____

12._____

13._____

14._____

15._____

16._____

17._____

18._____

19._____

20._____

Pick three from the list that you can do in the next week, and three more you can do in the next month. Share with your group and therapist. Commit to a date by when you will have done them. Record your reactions in your journal.

SHAME RECOVERY PLAN

An injury to one's sense of self forges some bonds. The self-injury becomes part of the fabric of the relationship and further disrupts the natural unfolding of the self. When this involves terror of any sort, an emptiness forms at the core of the person and the self becomes inconsolable. No addiction can fill it. No denial of self will restore it. No single gesture will be believable. Only a profound sense of the human community caring for the self can seal up this hole. We call this wound *shame*.

This part of your recovery agenda looks at how the relationship forced you to devalue the self, and plans for self-restoration to the human community. Start by making a list of how the relationship devalued you. Think of times you felt unworthy, embarrassed, flawed or ashamed. Make a list of ten sources of shame in the relationship.

Devaluation in the Relationship

Example: I did things to please my partner sexually—like send pictures of me nude to a men's magazine—that deeply embarrassed me.

1._____
2._____
3._____
4._____
5._____
6._____
7._____
8._____

9._____

10._____

Share the list with your group and therapist. Note in your journal the feelings that accompanied each entry to the list. Ask your group what you need to do to build support for yourself.

REPETITION RECOVERY PLAN

Addiction to the trauma, or *repetition compulsion,* means that the victim seeks situations that duplicate the original trauma. The victim seeks similar situations to resolve the original trauma, in part to reexperience all the reactions to it, and in part to live out the original "working model" for relationships created in the abuse experience.

The following exercise was given to me by Marilyn Murry, author of *Prisoner of Another War.*[3] I have modified it some for inclusion in this planning process. It is one of the best ways to understand repetition compulsion in your life and to change it. It does, however, require some effort. What follows are step-by-step instructions.

1. Find a large piece of newsprint. A standard size is 24" x 36" and can be found in tablet form at any office supply store. You will also need felt tip colored markers that you can write legibly with.
2. On the newsprint, draw a large oval that takes up most of the newsprint. About three-quarters of the way up, draw a dotted line across the oval as in the figure that follows:

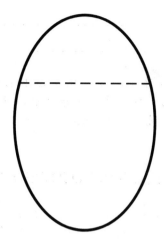

3. Outside of the oval and at the bottom of the page, write words that you think of when you think of your parents or original caregiver. Put the words you associate with Mom on the right and words you associate with Dad on the left. You only need five to ten words.

4. Now think of events in your life that were painful or difficult. Usually these are events in which there was profound disappointment, betrayal or abuse. Think of times when you were embarrassed or let down, or when there was some upset or crisis that involved you. Starting with the earliest events you can remember from early childhood, draw a small symbol for each event and separate it by a small curve, as in the figure that follows. Do not use words—only symbols.

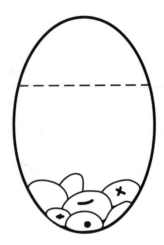

With all these events recorded, the bottom of your oval will start to look like a honeycomb. Keep adding events through the various phases of your life—preschool, elementary school, early teenage years, young adulthood and adulthood to the present. Fill the oval up to the dotted line. The most recent should be near the top and the earliest at the bottom. Done well, this should take many hours to complete.

5. Before going on to the next instructions, spend time showing your work to your therapist or your sponsor. Ask this person to look for themes that are common to the events. Examples would be: "Many of the events represent some type of abandonment" or "The events seem to indicate extreme neglect." When you have these repeating themes clear, proceed to the next step.

6. Outside of the oval, in the upper-right corner, list what roles you played in the family (such as hero, scapegoat, etc.). Outside of the oval, in the upper-left corner, list family rules that affected you (such as "don't show feelings," etc.).

7. On the basis of all this work, write what you believe your family's marching orders to you were. Write it in the form of a mission statement. This mission statement should accurately state what you perceived your family wanted you to do with your life. If you were the loyal kid, or the hero, what were you supposed to do in life? Record this mission statement in the top quarter of the oval, above the dotted line.

Your newsprint should end up looking like this:

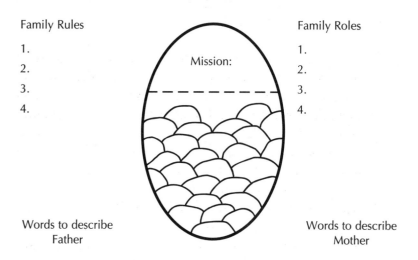

Family Rules

1.

2.

3.

4.

Mission:

Family Roles

1.

2.

3.

4.

Words to describe
Father

Words to describe
Mother

8. If you had the power to clone yourself—meaning the same you with no programming—what mission would you give yourself? Write that mission down. In your journal, respond to the following questions:

What does the mission given you by your family have to do with the trauma bond(s) in which you have been?

How did the original mission create repeated events throughout your life?

What are you willing to do in order to change the mission?

What steps would that take?

Who can help you with it?

How will you start?

Suggestion: In this task of changing the mission, there are two books designed to help you with that process. *The Artist's Way,* by Julia Cameron and *First Things First,* by Stephen Covey. I highly recommend both of them.

8

WHAT ARE THE RISKS OF RECOVERY?

To "own" one's shadow is the highest moral act of a human.

ROBERT JOHNSON

Some of us cried out, "It's too great a task!"

THE BIG BOOK OF ALCOHOLICS ANONYMOUS

Physicists tell us that once an atom has touched another atom, there is a relationship between the two atoms that endures forever, no matter how far they are from each other. While the physics involved are quite complex, the physical relationship principles are quite simple. Once made, a relationship always exists. It seems that in human relationships, that principle exists as well. Once a person has been part of our lives, the ripples remain, even though we have no further contact. In that sense a relationship continues even though we may consciously exorcise it from our conscious contact. Once you understand that principle, a shift will occur in all of your contact with others.

If the relationship was toxic, as in a traumatic bond, the relationship must go through a transformation, since it will be always with you. You do not need to be in contact with the person to change the nature of the relationship. You can change how you perceive it. You can change how it impacts you. This is true of all human systems—intact or not.

Some time ago I was responsible for a family-centered treatment center that took in all members of the family down to age six. Typically, we had twenty or more families attend at once. We often did an exercise with them that we described as a set of skills to teach problem solving. We started by having everyone line up against the wall according to age. We started with the youngest child and finished with the oldest adult. The youngest kids would then pick out new brothers and sisters from the older kids. These new "siblings" would then pick out new parents. We then taught the concept of "brainstorming" and "win-win" problem solving to these reconstituted families. Then, we gave the families a task or problem to solve. They were to spend the evening (three hours) doing something no one in this new family had ever done before. They typically went out and had a great time with each other.

When their therapists referred these families to us, they pointed out that the family members did not have skills in problem solving, boundary setting, intimacy or even play. Yet when you put these same people with other people's spouses and with other people's children, they had appropriate boundaries, solved problems, communicated effectively, could be vulnerable and could have fun. In fact, when they returned from the exercise the kids would ask, "Why can't our family have fun like this?" The adults, too, asked why it was so different. Their questions gave us the perfect opportunity to explain about systems and risk. It was not that they did not know how to be different with each other. They did know. It was more about risking being different.

So it is with traumatic relationships. Whether it be no

contact, limited contact or full relationship, there needs to be a shift. Your whole emotional and intellectual stance toward that person must be different. By this point you already have what you need to know. The problem of recovery is whether you are willing to risk the changes necessary. Those risks are as follows:

TO COMMIT TO REALITY AT ALL COSTS . . .

The movie *Mask* tells the story of a young man who had an illness that, among other things, "lionized" his face. His facial features were so distorted that they often repelled people. The movie tells the story of how he deals with other adolescents, his first girlfriend, other adults, his family and ultimately his death. There is a point in the story when the boy, his mother and their friends go to an amusement park and buy tickets to the fun house. In the fun house are the typical mirrors that distort appearance. The mirrors make you look fat or skinny or misshapen—only in the movie, the boy's face in the distorting mirror looks "normal." He calls his mother over to see. The poignancy of the scene comes with the two of them gazing at the handsome face he would have had without his illness.

In many ways, betrayal and exploitation are like being in the fun house. It makes the abnormal and the grotesque appear normal. Trauma distorts our perceptions just as sure as the mirrors in the fun house. Your task is to leave the fun house and face the reality without the distortion. This risk is the price of admission to recovery. You simply have to be willing to do it.

Scientists who studied trauma in rats made a startling discovery: Rats who received electric-shock treatment in little boxes returned to those little boxes when they experienced stress from other sources. Even though they received electrical shocks upon entering the boxes, they still returned to their boxes. It was a familiar, known way to return to their stress.

Similarly, the trauma-bonded survivor will run back into the fun house of exploitation even though it will be destructive.

Recovery requires staying in reality.

Betsy was a woman who finally chose reality. For four years, she was in a sexual relationship with a clergyman who was also her therapist. She knew it was wrong and destructive. She even went to the extent of getting another therapist two years into the relationship. When that therapist asked for the name of who it was that was exploiting her, she could not give up the name and eventually dropped out of therapy. Time and time again she tried to leave, but could not. She would run back to the minister, seduced by yet another story of how badly he was hurting. But finally she realized how crazy things were when she discovered that the clergyman and his wife were stalking her. She left therapy with the exploitive therapist. She told her support group and her children. It was the children that did it. When she saw how upset they were, she knew there was no going back. She had to make the break. When she came out publicly with her story, other women came forward. These other women joined her in reality. There was no going back for them, the congregation and the small town where they lived. The price of admission—reality.

THE MISPERCEPTIONS OF OTHERS

Once you have clarity about reality you must be willing to risk that others will misperceive you. Survivors want others to understand them. They do not want anyone upset with them. Their childhood training taught them that "if you cannot say something nice, do not say anything at all." If they have tried to change in the past they may even have had their lives threatened. They hold out a vain hope that they can write a letter to explain their actions or that they can have the "talk" that will gain them the acceptance of their actions. The fact is that they can give the perfect explanation and others in the abusive system will not understand it, maybe not even believe it. Even those who truly do cherish the survivor will misperceive. Remember, they are back in the fun house. If survivors are making significant changes, the people around them will not like it. They will misinterpret the survivor's actions. They may even question the survivor's motivation and conduct. Count on it.

The problem is shame. Shame is part of our internal guidance system, which tells us what is appropriate. Survivors embedded in traumatic shame become so other-directed that they lose their sense of self. They feel like the exploitation is their fault. The victim then carries the shame of the abuser and is shameful. The abuser, however, remains shameless. The victim becomes more desperate for the approval of others. For the victim, shame ceases to be a tool for appropriate action and becomes a prison from which there is a loss of autonomy and freedom.

When Betsy reported what happened to her with her minister-therapist, it became public. Members of the church she had attended for twenty years shunned her. People whom she thought were her friends and part of her spiritual support network would not talk with her. The parish issued a letter asking for prayers for the man who had abused her. When it mentioned her name it simply referred to her as "the cause of the problem." The church that had been her home abandoned her when she told the truth. Fortunately, Betsy had her support group and her new therapist. She knew that the congregation's shunning her was not so much about her as it was about its members' own issues—including the church's feelings of betrayal and pain. Remember, others in the system will have to go through denial, fear and anger before they get to the pain. That includes family members, friends and other people on whom survivors might count. If you are committed to reality, you must accept that people will misperceive you.

TO HAVE BOUNDARIES . . .

If you are willing to have others misperceive you, then you must run the risk of drawing boundaries. Implementing the boundaries you have specified in your recovery plan will upset people. With time, however, you will learn that not only is it alright for you to upset people but you also may learn to enjoy upsetting them. Sometimes you may set exaggerated boundaries, meaning that they are more rigid than the situation calls for. It makes no difference. The learning is in having them. It makes up for the years of deficits caused by having no boundaries at all.

The deeper issue with boundaries is that they force an essential restructuring of the relationship with self. The autonomy that you lost to shame is regained in several ways. First, within the exploitive system victims make promises to themselves that they do not keep. They will draw lines in the sand and say no more, then let people step over them with impunity. No one takes them seriously, which adds to their shame. When the victim starts insisting on maintaining limits and meeting her own needs, self-respect emerges. Here is a person who demands reckoning; a person of value.

Second, having boundaries clarifies values. They essentially are the answer to the question, "For what am I willing to fight?" Those values help define who the person is.

Finally, by successfully implementing boundaries, a new trust for yourself emerges. Victims learn that they do not have to have the zipper on the outside. They can and will take care of themselves, which creates a new sense of safety. For example, if one of the coping strategies for sexual trauma is to become celibate, having boundaries can be a revolution. You can be sexual and passionate if you know you will not let anyone exploit you. If you have good boundaries, no one can exploit you. By being trustworthy to yourself, you can give yourself over to passion. You know that you will take care of yourself. Perhaps the most important part of recovery is developing a trustworthy relationship with self.

TO SAY GOOD-BYE . . .

If someone does not respect your boundaries, you will have to leave. Many times I have witnessed incidents in which the victim gets to the point where she is ready to leave, only to have the abuser deliver the most compelling version of the seduction story. The abuser does not test the boundaries at that point, but once the victim is sucked back into the circle, the boundary abuse occurs again.

How can you change this? It is simple. State what is not acceptable and indicate that the cost of crossing the line will be that you will leave. For some people that is all that is necessary. When the line is crossed, you have your answer about the value of the relationship and the state of health of the other person. The best thing for you—and in fact the other person as well— is to face the reality that the relationship cannot survive.

Saying good-bye is wrenching for survivors, who already grieve their many losses. Here the survivor must confront the deep desire for the seduction story to be true. There is more than exploitation or abuse at stake here. There is the loss of some dream or core hope that made the seduction story so irresistible. Usually that dream or hope has roots in some original wound for which the survivor has not yet fully grieved. So when it is time for good-bye, the grief will be over-whelming. The only choice you have to survive is to embrace the pain and experience the loss. In many ways the betrayal bond protected you against that pain.

You may not have to say good-bye, but you must be willing to do so. In fact, life as you know it may require a complete transformation for you to survive these relationships. Work, values, homes, friends and even family relationships may have to substantively change for a successful recovery. What lengths are you willing to go to in order to be free? When you answer that question, you may have to face another risk: to be alone and be okay.

TO BE ALONE AND OKAY...

Behind grieving past losses lurks the fear of being alone. Yet it is the essential component of having a relationship with yourself. It is that sense of enjoying your own presence. We are not talking about narcissism here. We are describing the ability to be alone with yourself so you are clear about your own internal processes, your needs and your creative expression. For those who fear abandonment, the shift to a positive regard for oneself and the desire for time with oneself is one of the key developmental changes that an abusive environment may have blocked. Instead of shame, the survivor moves into autonomy. Theologian Henri Nouwen calls this transition the "conversion of loneliness into solitude."[1] Many people suffer terrible relationships because they fear being alone. They give themselves away piece by piece rather than face an empty house or apartment. They will accept partial relationships, as in:

> the leftover attention from a workaholic spouse
>
> the second-class status of mistress
>
> the secret, clandestine affair
>
> the partner to the addicted spouse
>
> the illegal, exploitive relationship
>
> the life of loving someone on the run
>
> the partner of the inmate in prison
>
> the long-distance relationship

Yet in these cases, something is *not* better than nothing. People who are not afraid to be alone can afford to demand relationships that work. They are not desperate while between relationships. Nor do they fill their lives with mindless television or mind-numbing addictions. They learn to be alone and be okay.

TO BE SPIRITUAL . . .

The following is a simple statement of what happens spiritually:

> Crisis and pain force surrender.
>
> We accept the realities we tried to flee.
>
> The lesson will be repeated until learned. If ignored, the lessons become harder.
>
> The lessons teach us about human limitation.
>
> We believed we were more than other humans. We could escape the harm.
>
> When we accept suffering, we reconnect with the deeper rhythms of the universe.
>
> We cannot escape the inevitable message. Now it means too much.
>
> We have lost too much, but we do have integrity.
>
> Never again will we let things not matter. We are part of a larger purpose.
>
> We know we have learned the lesson when our actions change.

Simple.

Nouwen describes three essential movements to a spiritual life. First comes the connection with self and the acceptance of your own brokenness. Then there is the acceptance of the community and a renewed trust of others. The ability to trust oneself and others clears the path to trusting a creator. That trust also means acceptance of a larger purpose, a purpose in which, at times, even bad things can happen to very good people.

For many survivors, the gateway to a spiritual life starts with a new relationship with oneself and with the growing network of relationships in the support community. To trust a higher purpose or power requires an essential trust of others. Trust of others really only comes with a deep trust of your own integrity. For example, will you follow through on enforcing the boundaries you have set? If you know you are untrustworthy, then it is difficult to take the next step of believing it possible that others can be trustworthy. Trusting a higher power, then, will remain elusive. Trust starts when you risk taking a stand. Then, somehow, it all matters. In the trauma bond you were unfaithful to yourself and so someone hurt you. By being true to yourself you will heal. And out of that healing a spiritual life emerges. It's amazing what betrayal can teach us if we are willing to learn.

TO BE HONEST . . .

If you have a solid spiritual life, you realize that nothing really disconnects you from others. Then it is a matter of courage to be yourself and to be honest about who you are. This means:

> to admit the hard things about yourself
>
> to be clear about hard things others must hear
>
> to not mislead anyone
>
> to not live a secret life
>
> to abandon false fronts and false pride

to be clear about your intent

to tell the truth

to not hide from difficult moments

to give up being "nice" all the time

to state your needs and wants without shame

to not cover or lie for anyone

The truth does, in fact, make you free.

TO BE VULNERABLE . . .

The most important skill to acquire and use in recovery is the capacity to get a consultation. To get a consultation means to involve people in what goes on in your own interior world. The dumb thoughts. The scary thoughts. The garbled thoughts. The irrational fears. The angry, vengeful fantasies. The nightmares. The unspoken desire. By sharing with others, you have an examined life. People know who you are. They also help you with their perspectives and ideas. They bring reality and problem-solving skills to your life. This process allows for integration of the darker side of yourself and acceptance of your humanness.

For the survivor whose vulnerability has been exploited, this risk may first appear insurmountable. It is from the sharing of stories, however, that trust starts to build. Common experience reduces the isolation of shame. It is then that we can share the shadow side of ourselves, the nasty, mean-spirited side of ourselves, the side that others have victimized, the side whose motives for rescuing were not that wonderful, the side that has frightening fantasies. Failure to own that reality will keep us from the serenity we seek. Disowning our shadow will prevent integrity. Remember that others are mirrors for ourselves. What we love or hate in others reflects what we love or hate about ourselves. Dr. Carl Jung wrote that to acknowledge our skeletons is the only way we will be able to ultimately accept the "gold" of life. More important, he observed that the greatest gift you could give your children (and the next generation) is to acknowledge the shadow side of yourself. To do that means to be vulnerable.[2]

TO FIGHT...

Most survivors avoid conflict. In their past, anger and violence meant great danger. There were the rules about keeping the peace and saying nice things. The truth is that sometimes you will have to fight. To remove yourself from a trauma bond safely and with self-care might mean you have to insist on your rights. Do not accept a significant loss because it is easier not to fight for it. You may need to get help to coach you, to advocate for you or even to represent you. But it is okay to get what is yours, what you need or what others should do for you. It is also important to let go of being nice. It is always important to let others hear you. It is always important to protect yourself. It is always important to make sure you do not intentionally hurt others purely for the sake of hurting them. These are all good reasons to fight. Besides, the boundaries become clear in the process.

Remember that adversarial processes such as court action can also be traumatic. As I indicated earlier, anger can lead to negative intimacy. Your goal should be to take care of yourself and not to allow the bond to reseduce you.

Also, all intimacy has some struggle to it. There is no healthy relationship that does not have significant differences in it. That is why I like the fair fight contract that Recovering Couples Anonymous uses. Learning to handle differences safely is the most important skill a couple can have. It is more important than love, attraction and common interests. Sustained intimacy will only last if the couple can learn to be separate *and* together. Working that through will happen over and over again. If it is a safe process, there will be joy. The same principles apply to raising children, having friends and forging successful work relationships. And yes, it applies to relationships with therapists as well.

TO DEFINE SELF...

One of the most common reports from people emerging from a trauma bond is that they had not realized how much someone else regulated their values, lifestyle and daily choices. The people in most of the situations described in this book probably said the phrase, "He (she) took over my life." Once out of the trauma bond, even the most simple things can become difficult. I had one woman describe for me how simply decorating her new apartment became a challenge. She wanted the apartment to be a statement about who she had become, but it was a challenge—since even she was still unclear about that.

Sometimes the dilemmas are heart wrenching; they are more akin to the level of problem that Orestes faced. If you remember, Orestes had to choose between avenging his father's death and murdering his mother. I have seen too many situations such as that, situations for which there were no easy solutions.

Consider Tom, whose situation with his volatile wife Barbara I described in chapter 5. One of Tom's core values was to be the best parent he knew how to be to his children. His divorce settled with a joint custody arrangement, which featured the children going back and forth between the two homes at biweekly intervals. While Tom got much better at limiting Barbara's intrusions in his life, she still caused what he called "emotional overhead." Just as a business has overhead costs, having to be a parent with Barbara cost Tom a certain amount of chaos. While he couldn't eliminate the chaos entirely, he knew he had to get some physical distance between Barbara and himself. When he received an extraordinary job offer, 1,500 miles away, he was elated. But what about the children? The older kids were old enough that he did not worry about his relationship with them. But the youngest was an ache in his heart. She did not want to move, and that meant staying with Barbara. So his choice was to pass on the offer and stay with the kids, or be true to himself and accept the incredible offer he received.

He accepted the offer and learned much. He was like a new man. He felt more like himself than he had in years. He became CEO of the company. He remarried. Two of his children actually moved in with him while they went to college and graduate school; one of them was his youngest child.

Tom remained true to himself and doing so paid off for him. The price? A soul-wrenching choice that offered no guarantees.

You may experience terrible choices on your recovery path. They will force you to define who you are and what you are all about.

Expect the difficult.

TO TAKE RESPONSIBILITY FOR YOURSELF...

This risk reminds me of how monkeys are captured in Africa. Tribal peoples put out slotted cages filled with fresh fruit. The cages are anchored securely to the ground. Monkeys discover the cages, reach in and grab the fruit. Of course, they cannot retrieve the fruit because as long as the hand holds the fruit, it will not fit through the bars of the cage. The monkeys are then trapped. They could always let go of the fruit and escape, but they refuse to let go. Even as their human captors pick them up, they hold on.

Trauma bonds are similar. There is always something kind, noble or redeeming about someone who has betrayed you.

Victims of betrayal will hold to those good things even while the world crashes in around them. By holding on they stay stuck, just like the monkeys. We do make our own prisons.

That is exactly how it was with Jack. He sat in my office, admitted for an addiction relapse and treatment because he was absolutely suicidal about a woman he had broken up with four months earlier. He was a very high-profile sports figure. He spent over a half-hour telling me how she was his dream woman. The sex was fabulous. She was his best friend. They each had children the same ages who really got along well with one another. They had been together for two years. All of which was well and good, except that she had stolen thirty thousand dollars from him, embarrassed him countless times with violent outbursts at highly visible public events, alienated all of his friends, and kept him in constant turmoil with her dramatic exits. After their last breakup she became involved with one of his closest colleagues and slept with him within the week. Jack was sad she would no longer take his calls. I told him he was lucky, and therapy began.

The scenarios of abuse in Jack's history and her history were there. He admitted that she terrified him most of the time. And he acknowledged that the relationship was over. Yet he had a thread of hope he could get her to therapy and retrieve the relationship. Like a monkey with fruit, Jack was holding on to the dream.

The bottom line is: *Your life is up to you. Take charge of it or somebody else will.*

FROM SUFFERING TO MEANING . . .

There is a revolution occurring. Sometimes it is public and the battle lines are clearly drawn. Sometimes it is very personal and the lines are very intimate. The struggle goes on in courtrooms, corporate offices, legislatures, universities and playgrounds. It affects employers, parents, spouses, teachers, judges and members of the clergy. Many of us think it is a turning point for our species. The revolution is about relationships. Whether it is betrayal by seduction, terror, power, intimacy or spirit, exploitation is simply no longer acceptable. We've surveyed centuries of damage and we know better. We need to move toward a culture of mutuality and respect. We can build our relationships on the basis of our competencies, needs and care. Men and women need to share power and privilege. All of us must commit to the nurturing of children. And we are accountable to each other for our behavior. There is no more room for terror in the human community.

Ecologically, we are now too numerous to continue to abuse the planet. We must deeply acknowledge our connections with all creatures. We must now respect that interdependence or we will suffer greatly. While most of us know that danger, the abuse of the earth still continues. Our consciousness must eventually outstrip the forces of exploitation. Similarly, we understand what trauma does. Violence simply begets more violence. War, child abuse, domestic violence, sexual harassment and all manner of exploitation limit what we can be. In fact, one of the most astute observers about childhood over time, Lloyd deMause, writes, "The history of childhood is a nightmare from which we have only recently begun to awaken."[3] Just as with with our ecological awareness, the fact that we are awake does not mean the abuse has stopped.

I wish to applaud you, dear reader, for completing this book and meeting all its demands. For you have gone beyond awareness. You have committed yourself to stopping or changing an abusive relationship. In that you have helped all of us. You have contributed in the only way any of us can make a difference. You were not one of those who found the risks too great a task. Good work.

I have included a final metaphor at the end of this chapter to take with you on your journey. My best wishes go with you.

A GUIDED IMAGERY FOR THE JOURNEY . . .

The following is a guided imagery that has been used by thousands of recovering people. Once you learn the structure of it, you can use it over and over again to help you reclaim your priorities. You can have a friend read it to you or even ask your therapist to do it with you. Some have recorded it then played the tape for themselves. A special version of this imagery is on an audiocassette tape, prepared by the author, entitled *Reclaiming Yourself.* You can order the tape by calling 800-955-9853 or writing New Freedom Publications, P.O. Box 3345, Wickenburg, Arizona, 85358.

Guided imageries are not magic. They are metaphors that help you access your own wisdom. Each time you use the imagery you will come up with new insights. This particular imagery is very easy to use because all you have to know is the directions of north, south, east and west. Native Americans would use these directions as a way to inventory where they were in their life's journey. We can use the same process as well.

To do this you will need a sanctuary or safe place. Think of some location in your life that has been very peaceful and serene for you. Picture that as the site for this imagery. Now, simply follow the instructions.

Close your eyes and make yourself comfortable. Make sure nothing physical distracts you. If you are upset about any-thing, picture a box around it and set it aside. Tune in now to your own bodily rhythms—your breathing and your heart beating. Know that with each beat of your heart and each breath that you take, you are participating in the larger forces of the universe. Each heartbeat and each breath is therefore sacred.

Imagine a safe place. A place that has no demands. A place that always gives peace. Look around the safe place. Notice colors, sounds and textures. What is it that makes this place so good for you?

You become aware of another presence in the safe place. You look to see who it is. It is a healer, a wise person who has come to support you in the safe place. Greet your healer. Your healer invites you to do an inventory of your life but wishes to do it in the manner of traditional peoples. Your healer then asks you to face the north and joins you at your side.

North is the direction of the winter winds. It is the direction of challenge, endurance and courage. Your healer asks for what challenge do you need to be strong? What do you need courage to face? Tell your healer what that is. Your healer then asks you to face the East.

East is the direction of the rising sun. It is the direction of beginnings. Your healer asks what do you need to start in your life? When is it time to begin? Tell your healer what you must begin. Your healer then asks you to face the south.

South is the direction of the summer sun. It is the direction of nurturing, vitality and growth. Your healer asks what do you have going on in your life that needs your attention, your nurturing, your cultivation? What do you need to grow or heal? Tell your healer what you must have now in order to grow. Your healer then asks you to face the west.

West is the direction of the setting sun. It is the direction of endings. Your healer asks what do you need to bring to a close? To whom do you need to say goodbye? Tell your healer what you have not been willing to end and that you know it is time now to end it. Your healer then asks you to gaze upward to Father Sky.

The sky is the direction of openness and possibility. It is the direction of creativity. Your healer asks you to picture yourself against the sky doing something that uses talents you currently do not use. Tell your healer about your unused talents. Your healer then asks you to gaze downward toward Mother Earth.

Mother Earth is the direction of gravity. It is the direction of stability. Your healer asks what is it that you need to remain stable? Tell your healer what you need to remain grounded. Sit down with your healer. Your healer has a special message for you about your direction in life. What does your healer tell you?

As you talk, you become aware of another presence in the safe place. As you look to see who it is, you see that it is a child about five years old. As the child approaches, you realize the child is you at the age of five. Welcome the child. Ask the child how things are going. What concerns and fears does the child have? Allow the child to climb into your lap. Reassure the child. Even though the child has maybe suffered neglect, or harm, or abandonment, or even abuse, you are now here to protect the child. You will allow nothing to happen to the child. Hold the child close and comfort the child. As you hold the child in your arms, the healer now has something to tell you about the child. What does the healer say?

As you and the healer talk, the child becomes restless. The child gets up and asks if you and the healer would like to play. You and the healer agree. You take one hand and the healer takes the other and you leave the safe place. You walk out into a spectacular green meadow. At one end of the meadow is a playground with all kinds of play equipment: water slides, merry-go-rounds, jungle gyms and swings. Picture yourself playing. Notice that you can have intense feelings and still play.

You realize it is time to leave. Tell the child and the healer you have to go. The child responds, "We know. But first we have a gift for you." The child runs and gets the gift and hands it to you. If it is wrapped, unwrap it. What is the gift? What does it look like? What does it mean? Thank the child and the healer. And when you are ready, open your eyes.

This imagery has helped many survivors sort out their needs. Once you have done it, simply remember what happens with each direction: with the north, cold winds; with the east, the day's beginning; with the south, growth due to the summer sun; the west, day's end; the sky, openness and creativity; and the earth, gravity and stability. After a while you will not need the script. You will be able to do it on your own.

As before, use your journal to record your imagery. What emerged for you with each direction? What happened with the healer and the child? How was it to play? What was the gift? Record what insights you have gained and share with your therapist and group.

Appendix: Resources

General

Al-Anon Family Group Headquarters, Inc. (AFG), and
Alateen
P.O. Box 862
Midtown Station
New York, NY 10018-0862
(212) 302-7240
(800) 356-9996
(212) 869-3757 fax

Alcohol and Drug Problems Association of North America
1555 Wilson Boulevard
Suite 300
Arlington, VA 22209
(703) 875-8684

Alcoholics Anonymous World Services
475 Riverside Drive
New York, NY 10163
(212) 870-3400

AMEND (Domestic Violence)
777 Grant Street
Suite 600
Denver, CO 80203
(303) 832-6363

Amnesty International of the USA (AIUSA)
322 8th Avenue
New York, NY 10001
(212) 807-1451
(800) AMNESTY
(212) 627-1451 fax

BA (Batterers Anonymous)
1850 N. Riverside, Avenue, No. 220
Rialto, CA 92376
(909) 355-1100

Co-Dependents Anonymous
P.O. Box 33577
Phoenix, AZ 85067-3577
(602) 277-7991

GAM-ANON International
P.O. Box 157
Whitestone, NY 11357
(718) 352-1671

Gamblers Anonymous
P.O. Box 17173
Los Angeles, CA 90010
(213) 386-8789

National Catholic Council on Alcoholism and Related
Drug Problems (NCCA)
1550 Hendrickson Street
Brooklyn, NY 11234-3514
(718) 951-7177

National Coalition Against Domestic Violence (NCADV)
P.O. Box 18749
Denver, CO 80218
(303) 839-1852

National Council for Couple and Family Recovery
(NCCFR)
434 Lee Avenue
St Louis, MO 63119
(314) 963-8898

National Council on Alcoholism and Drug Dependence
12 W. 21st Street
New York, NY 10010

National Council on Sexual Addiction and Compulsivity
(NCSAC)
1090 Northchase Parkway
Suite 200 South
Marietta, GA 30067
(770) 989-9754

Overeaters Anonymous
6075 Zenith Court NE
Rio Rancho, NM 87124-6424
(505) 891-2664

Parents Anonymous
675 W. Foothill Boulevard
Suite 220
Claremont, CA 91711-3416
(909) 621-6184

Parents United International (PUI)
615 15th Street
Modesto, CA 953354-2510
(408) 453-7616
(408) 453-9064 fax

Recovering Couples Anonymous (RCA)
P.O. Box 11872
St Louis, MO 63105
(314) 830-2600

Cults

Cult Awareness Network (CAN)
2421 W. Pratt Boulevard
Suite 1173
Chicago, IL 60645
(312) 267-7777

Sex Addiction

COSA
9337-B Katy Freeway
Suite 142
Houston, TX 77024

Incest Survivors Anonymous
P.O. Box 17245
Long Beach, CA 90807-7245
(310) 428-5599

Incest Survivors Resource Network International (ISRNI)
P.O. Box 7375
Las Cruces, NM 88006
(505) 521-4260
(505) 521-3723 fax

Sex Addicts Anonymous (SAA)
P.O. Box 3038   P.O. Box 70949
Minneapolis, MN 55403   Houston, TX 77270
(612) 339-0217   (713) 869-4902

Sexaholics Anonymous (SA)
P.O. Box 111910
Nashville, TN 37222-1910
(615) 331-6230

Sex and Love Addicts Anonymous (SLAA)
The Augustine Fellowship
P.O. Box 650010
West Newton, MA 02165-0010
(617) 332-1845

Sexual Compulsive Anonymous (SCA)
P.O. Box 1585
Old Chelsea Station
New York, NY 10011
(212) 439-1123

Survivors of Incest Anonymous (SIA)
P.O. Box 21817
Baltimore, MD 21222
(410) 282-3400

Notes

Introduction: Why Read This Book?

1. J. Bain, *Ontario Medical Review* (January 1989): 20–49.

2. Alice Miller, *For Your Own Good* (New York: Farrar, Straus & Giroux, Inc., 1983).

Chapter 2: Trauma Bonds and Their Allies

1. John Money, Ph.D., Charles Annecillo, Sc.D., and June Werlwas Hutchison, M.M.H., "Forensic and Family Psychiatry in Abuse Dwarfism: Munchausen's Syndrome by Proxy, Atonement, and Addiction to Abuse," *Journal of Sex and Marital Therapy* 11 no. 1, (Spring 1985): 35.

2. Bessel van der Kolk, "The Trauma Spectrum: The Interaction of Biological and Social Events in the Genesis of the Trauma Response," *Journal of Traumatic Stress* 1, no. 3 (1988): 286. See also Bessel van der Kolk, "The Compulsion to Repeat the Trauma," *Journal of Victims of Sexual Abuse* 12 (1989): 389.

3. Dee L. R. Graham with Edna I. Rawlings and Roberta K. Rigsby, *Loving to Survive* (New York: New York University Press, 1994).

4. Martin Gilbert, *The Boys* (New York: Henry Holt and Company, 1997).

Chapter 3: What Does Betrayal Do to Relationships?

1. See Bessel van der Kolk, "The Trauma Spectrum: The Interaction of Biological and Social Events in the Genesis of the Trauma Response," *Journal of Traumatic Stress* 1 (1988): 286, and Bessel van der Kolk, "The Compulsion to Repeat Trauma," *Journal of Victims of Sexual Abuse* 12 (1989): 389. See also Andrine M. Lemieu, M.A. and Christopher L. Coe, Ph.D., "Abuse-Related Post-Traumatic Stress Disorder: Evidence for Chronic Neuroendocrine Activation in Women," *Psychosomatic Medicine* 57 (1995): 105.

2. Amanda Vogt, "Cults Get Mainstream Makeover," *The Arizona Republic* 26 April 1997, sec. R, p. 2.

3. Two examples of this type of research can be found in Renee L. Binder, M.D., "Why Women Don't Report Sexual Assault," *Journal of Clinical Psychiatry* 42, no. 11 (1981): 437, and Thomas G. Gutheil, M.D., "Patients Involved in Sexual Misconduct with Therapists: Is a Victim Profile Possible?," *Psychiatric Annals* 21, no. 11 (1991): 661.

4. Dara A. Charney, M.D., C.M. and Ruth C. Russell, M.D., C.M., F.R.C.P., "An Overview of Sexual Harassment," *American Journal of Psychiatry* 151, no. 1 (1994): 10.

5. Patricia A. Gwartney-Gibbs and Denise H. Lach, "Sociological Explanation for Failure to Seek Sexual Harassment Remedies," *Mediation Quarterly* 9 (1992): 365.

6. Mary De Young and Judith A. Lowry, "Traumatic Bonding: Clinical Implications in Incest," *Child Welfare League of America* LXXI (1992): 165–175.

7. For elaboration of this concept see White, William L., *Incest in the Organizational Family* (Bloomington, Ill.: The Lighthouse Training Institute, 1986).

8. E. Burkett and F. Bruni, *A Gospel of Shame: Child Sexual Abuse and the Catholic Church* (New York: Viking, 1993).

9. M. M. Fortune, *Is Nothing Sacred? When Sex Invades the Pastoral Relationship* (San Francisco: HarperCollins, 1989).

10. J. Berry, *Lead Us Not into Temptation: Catholic Priests and the Sexual Abuse of Children* (New York: Doubleday, 1992).

11. Richard A.W. Sipe, *Sex, Priests and Power: Anatomy of a Crisis* (New York: Brunner/Mazel, Inc., 1995).

12. Anson Shupe, *In the Name of All That Is Holy* (Greenwood, Conn.: Praeger Publishers, 1995). See also G. R. Schoener, J. C. Milgrom, E. T. Luepker, and R. M. Conroe, *Psychotherapists' Sexual Involvement with Clients* (Minneapolis: Minneapolis Walk-In Counseling Center, 1989), G. Gabbard, *Sexual Exploitation in Professional Relationships* (Washington, D.C.: American Psychiatric Press, 1989), and Richard Irons, M.D. and Mark Laaser, Ph.D., "The Abduction of Fidelity: Sexual Exploitation by Clergy—Experience with Inpatient Assessment," *Sexual Addiction and Compulsivity: The Journal of Treatment and Prevention* 1, no. 2 (1994): 119–129.

13. K. Lebacqz and R. G. Barton, *Sex in the Parish* (Louisville, Ky.: Westminster, 1991).

14. J. Seat, J. Trent, and K. Jwa, *Journal of Pastoral Care* 47 (Winter 1993): 363–370.

15. K. S. Leong, "Sexual Attraction and Misconduct Between Christian Therapists and Their Clients," *Dissertation Abstracts International* 50 (1989), 4225B.

16. Barbara R. McLaughlin, "Devastated Spirituality: The Impact of Clergy Sexual Abuse on the Survivor's Relationship with God and the Church," *Sexual Addiction and Compulsivity: The Journal of Treatment and Prevention* 1, no. 2 (1994): 145–158.

Chapter 4: What Makes Trauma Bonds Stronger?

1. American Medical Association, *Diagnostic and Treatment Guidelines on Domestic Violence* (Chicago: American Medical Association, 1992).

2. Mary De Young and Judith Lowry, "Traumatic Bonding: Clinical Implications in Incest," *Child Welfare League of America* LXXI (1992): 165–175.

3. Richard Irons, M.D. and Mark Laaser, Ph.D., "The Abduction of Fidelity: Sexual Exploitation by Clergy—Experience with Inpatient Assessment," *Sexual Addiction and Compulsivity: The Journal of Treatment and Prevention* 1, no. 2 (1994): 119–129.

4. Richard Solomon, "The Opponent-Process Theory of Acquired Motivation: The Costs of Pleasure and the Benefits of Pain," *American Psychologist* 35: 691–712.

5. For a good summary of this position see McClelland in Richard Lyons, "Stress Addiction," *New York Times*, 26 July: sec. C, p. 1.

6. Thomas Wolfe, *The Bonfire of the Vanities* (New York: Farrar, Straus & Giroux, Inc., 1987).

7. Robert M. Post, M.D., "Transduction of Psychosocial Stress into the Neurobiology of Recurrent Affective Disorder," *American Journal of Psychiatry* 149, no. 8 (1992): 999–1010.

8. Jerry Kroth, "Recapitulating Jonestown," *The Journal of Psychohistory* 11, no. 3 (1984): 385. See also Jose I. Lasaga, Ph.D., "Death in Jonestown: Techniques of Political Control by a Paranoid Leader," *Suicide and Life-Threatening Behavior* 10, no. 4 (1980), 210–213, Richard H. Seiden Hoyt, Ph.D. M.P.H., "Reverend Jones on Suicide," *Suicide and Life-Threatening Behavior* 9, no. 2 (1979): 116–119, and Albert Black Jr., Ph.D., "Jonestown—Two Faces of Suicide: A Durkheimian Analysis," *Suicide and Life-Threatening Behavior* 20, no. 4 (1990): 285–306.

9. William L. White, *Incest in the Organizational Family* (Bloomington, Ill.: The Lighthouse Training Institute, 1986): 108–109.

10. Bessel van der Kolk, "The Trauma Spectrum: The Interaction of Biological and Social Events in the Genesis of the Trauma Response," *Journal of Traumatic Stress* 1, no. 3 (1988): 273–290, and John Money, Ph.D., "Forensic and Family Psychiatry in Abuse Dwarfism: Munchausen's Syndrome by Proxy, Atonement and Addiction to Abuse, *Journal of Sex and Marital Therapy* 11, no. 1 (Spring 1985): 30–40.

11. For original research plus a review of this literature see Leslie L. Feinauer, "Comparison of Long-Term Effects of Child Abuse by Type of Abuse and by Relationship of the Offender and the Victim," *The American Journal of Family Therapy* 17, no. 1 (1989): 48–56.

12. Stephen B. Karpman, M.D., "Overlapping Egograms," *Transactional Analysis Journal* 4, no. 4 (October 1974): 16–19.

Chapter 5: What Is the Path of Awareness?

1. Charles Whitfield, "Denial of the Truth: Individual and Political Dysfunction in the Thomas-Hill Hearings," *The Journal of Psychohistory* 19, no. 3 (1992): 269–279.

2. David Calof, "Adult Survivors of Incest and Child Abuse, Part One: The Family Inside the Adult Child," *Family Therapy Today* 3 (1988): 1–5.

3. Ruth A. Blizard and Ann M. Bluhm, "Attachment to the Abuser: Integrating Object-Relations and Trauma Theories in Treatment of Abuse Survivors," *Psychotherapy* 31, no. 3 (1994): 383. See also K. Blum, M. Trachtenberg, and G. Kozlowski, "Cocaine Therapy: The Reward Cascade Link, *Professional Counselor* (January/February 1989): 27–30, 52.

4. For example of trauma-based compulsive-relationship behavior research see Malcolm West, Ph.D. and Adrienne E. R. Sheldon, B.A., "Classification of Pathological Attachment Patterns in Adults," *Journal of Personality Disorders* 2, no. 2 (1988): 153–159.

5. See chapter 5 of Patrick J. Carnes, *Don't Call It Love* (New York: Bantam Books, 1991) for data on codependency.

6. M. Scott Peck, *The Road Less Traveled* (New York: Simon & Schuster, 1978), 51, 295.

Chapter 6: What Is the Path of Action?

1. For review of this literature and model of the *testimony method* see Inger Agger, "Sexual Torture of Political Prisoners: An Overview," *Journal of Traumatic Stress* 2, no. 3 (1989): 305–318.

2. The classic book on that process is David Gordon, *Therapeutic Metaphors* (Cupertino, Calif.: Meta Publications, 1978).

3. Rochelle A. Scheela, "The Remodeling Process: A Grounded Theory Study of Perceptions of Treatment Among Adult Male Incest Offenders, *Journal of Offender Rehabilitation* 18, no. 3/4:167–189.

4. The concept of *carried shame* is described in Pia Mellody, Andrea Wells Miller, and J. Keith Miller, *Facing Codependency* (San Francisco: HarperCollins, 1989).

5. The zipper metaphor comes from M. Fossum and M. Mason, *Facing Shame: Families in Recovery* (New York: The Guilford Press, 1986).

Chapter 7: Further Steps on the Path to Recovery

1. Bessel van der Kolk, "The Trauma Spectrum: The Interaction of Biological and Social Events in the Genesis of the Trauma Response," *Journal of Traumatic Stress* 1, no. 3 (1988): 58.

2. Mario Puzo, *The Last Don* (New York: Random House, 1996).

3. Marilyn Murry, *Prisoner of Another War* (Berkeley, Calif.: Page Mill Press, 1991).

Chapter 8: What Are the Risks of Recovery?

1. Henri J. M. Nouwen, *Reaching Out* (New York: Doubleday & Company, 1975).

2. For an analysis of Jung around this issue see Robert Johnson, "On the Teeter-Totter of Ego," *Parabola: Myth, Tradition and the Search for Meaning: The Shadow* (Summer 1997): 19–25.

3. Lloyd DeMause, "The History of Child Abuse," *Sexual Addiction and Compulsivity* 1, no. 1 (1994): 77–91.

Bibliography

General References

American Medical Association. *Diagnostic and Treatment Guidelines on Domestic Violence.* Chicago: American Medical Association, 1992.

Bain, J. *Ontario Medical Review.* (January 1989): 20–49.

Berry, J. *Lead Us Not into Temptation: Catholic Priests and the Sexual Abuse of Children.* New York: Doubleday, 1992.

Binder, Renee L., M.D. "Why Women Don't Report Sexual Assault." *Journal of Clinical Psychiatry* 42, no. 11 (1981): 437.

Black, Albert Jr., Ph.D. "Jonestown—Two Faces of Suicide: A Durkheimian Analysis." *Suicide and Life-Threatening Behavior* 20, no. 4 (1990): 285–306.

Burkett, E., and F. Bruni. *A Gospel of Shame: Child Sexual Abuse and the Catholic Church.* New York: Viking, 1993.

Calof, David. "Adult Survivors of Incest and Child Abuse, Part One: The Family Inside the Adult Child." *Family Therapy Today* 3 (1988): 1–5.

Carnes, Patrick J., Ph.D. *Don't Call It Love.* New York: Bantam Books, 1991.

Charney, Dara A., M.D., C.M., and Ruth C. Russell, M.D., C.M., F.R.C.P. "An Overview of Sexual Harassment." *American Journal of Psychiatry* 151, no. 1 (1994): 10.

DeMause, Lloyd. "The History of Child Abuse." *Sexual Addiction and Compulsivity* 1, no. 1 (1994): 77–91.

Fortune, M. M. *Is Nothing Sacred? When Sex Invades the Pastoral Relationship.* San Francisco: HarperCollins, 1989.

Fossum, M., and M. Mason. *Facing Shame: Families in Recovery.* New York: The Guilford Press, 1986.

Gabbard, G. *Sexual Exploitation in Professional Relationships.* Washington, D.C.: American Psychiatric Press, 1989.

Gordon, David. *Therapeutic Metaphors.* Cupertino, Calif.: Meta Publications, 1978.

Gutheil, Thomas G., M.D. "Patients Involved in Sexual Misconduct with Therapists: Is a Victim Profile Possible?" *Psychiatric Annals* 21, no. 11 (1991): 661.

Gwartney-Gibbs, Patricia A., and Denise H. Lach. "Sociological Explanation for Failure to Seek Sexual Harassment Remedies." *Mediation Quarterly* 9 (1992): 365.

Hoyt, Richard H. Seiden, Ph.D., M.P.H. "Reverend Jones on Suicide." *Suicide and Life-Threatening Behavior* 9, no. 2 (1979): 116–119.

Johnson, Robert. "On the Teeter-Totter of Ego." *Parabola: Myth, Tradition and the Search for Meaning: The Shadow* (Summer 1997): 19–25.

Karpman, Stephen B., M.D. "Overlapping Egograms." *Transactional Analysis Journal* 4, no. 4 (October 1974): 16–19.

Kroth, Jerry. "Recapitulating Jonestown." *The Journal of Psychohistory* 11, no. 3 (1984): 385.

Lasaga, Jose I., Ph.D. "Death in Jonestown: Techniques of Political Control by a Paranoid Leader." *Suicide and Life-Threatening Behavior* 10, no. 4 (1980): 210–213.

Lebacqz, K., and R. G. Barton. *Sex in the Parish.* Louisville, Ky.: Westminster, 1991.

Leong, K. S. "Sexual Attraction and Misconduct Between Christian Therapists and Their Clients." *Dissertation Abstracts International* 50 (1989): 4225B.

McLaughlin, Barbara R. "Devastated Spirituality: The Impact of Clergy Sexual Abuse on the Survivor's Relationship with God and the Church." *Sexual Addiction and Compulsivity: The Journal of Treatment and Prevention* 1, no. 2 (1994): 145–158.

Mellody, Pia, Andrea Wells Miller, and J. Keith Miller. *Facing Codependency.* San Francisco: HarperCollins, 1989.

Nouwen, Henri J. M. *Reaching Out.* New York: Doubleday & Company, 1975.

Ochberg, Frank M., M.D. *Post-Traumatic Therapy and Victims of Violence.* New York: Brunner/Mazel, 1988.

Ochberg, Frank M., and David A. Soskis. *Victims of Terrorism.* Boulder, Colo.: Westview Press, 1982.

Peck, M. Scott. *The Road Less Traveled.* New York: Simon & Schuster, 1978.

Post, Robert M., M.D. "Transduction of Psychosocial Stress into the Neurobiology of Recurrent Affective Disorder." *American Journal of Psychiatry* 149, no. 8 (1992): 999–1010.

Puzo, Mario. *The Last Don.* New York: Random House, 1996.

Scheela, Rochelle A. "The Remodeling Process: A Grounded Theory Study of Perceptions of Treatment Among Adult Male Incest Offenders." *Journal of Offender Rehabilitation* 18, no. 3/4, 167–189.

Schoener, G. R., J. C. Milgrom, E. T. Luepker, and R. M. Conroe. *Psychotherapists' Sexual Involvement with Clients.* Minneapolis: Minneapolis Walk-In Counseling Center, 1989.

Shupe, Anson. *In the Name of All That Is Holy.* Greenwood, Conn.: Praeger Publishers, 1995.

Sipe, Richard A.W. *Sex, Priests and Power: Anatomy of a Crisis.* New York: Brunner/Mazel, 1995.

van der Kolk, Bessel. "The Trauma Spectrum: The Interaction of Biological and Social Events in the Genesis of the Trauma Response." *Journal of Traumatic Stress* 1, no. 3 (1988), 286.

———. *Traumatic Stress.* New York: The Guilford Press, 1996.

White, William L. *Incest in the Organizational Family.* Bloomington, Ill.: The Lighthouse Training Institute, 1986: 108–109.

Whitfield, Charles. "Denial of the Truth: Individual and Political Dysfunction in the Thomas-Hill Hearings." *The Journal of Psychohistory* 19, no. 3 (1992): 269–279.

Wolfe, Thomas. *The Bonfire of the Vanities*. New York: Farrar, Straus & Giroux, Inc., 1987.

Trauma Reactions

Agger, Inger. "Sexual Torture of Political Prisoners: An Overview." *Journal of Traumatic Stress* 2, no. 3 (1989): 305–318.

Briere, John. *Child Abuse Trauma: Theory and Treatment of the Lasting Effects*. Newbury Park: SAGE Publications, 1992.

Courtois, Christine. *Healing the Incest Wound: Adult Survivors in Therapy*. New York: W. W. Norton & Company, 1988.

Dolan, Yvonne. *Resolving Sexual Abuse: Solution-Focused Therapy and Ericksonian Hypnosis for Adult Survivors*. New York: W. W. Norton & Company, 1991.

Gilbert, Martin. *The Boys*. New York: Henry Holt and Company, 1997.

Grove, David, and B. I. Panzer. *Resolving Traumatic Memories: Metaphors and Symbols in Psychotherapy*. New York: Irvington Publishers, Inc., 1991.

Money, John, Ph.D., Charles Annecillo, Sc.D., and June Werlwas Hutchison, M.M.H. "Forensic and Family Psychiatry in Abuse Dwarfism: Munchausen's Syndrome by Proxy, Atonement, and Addiction to Abuse." *Journal of Sex and Marital Therapy* 11, no. 1 (Spring 1985): 30–40.

Murry, M. *Prisoner of Another War*. Berkeley, Calif.: Page Mill Press, 1991.

van der Kolk, Bessel. "The Trauma Spectrum: The Interaction of Biological and Social Events in the Genesis of the Trauma Response." *Journal of Traumatic Stress* 1, no. 3 (1988): 273–90.

———. "The Compulsion to Repeat the Trauma." *Journal of Victims of Sexual Abuse* 12 (1989): 389.

Trauma Pleasure

Anderson, Nancy B., M.A., and Eli J. Coleman, Ph.D. "Childhood Abuse and Family Sexual Attitudes in Sexually Compulsive Males: A Comparison of Three Clinical Groups." *American Journal of Preventive Psychiatry and Neurology on Medical Aspects of Sexual Addiction/ Compulsivity* (Spring 1991).

Blum, K., M. Trachtenberg, and G. Kozlowski. "Cocaine Therapy: The Reward Cascade Link." *Professional Counselor* (January/February 1989): 27–30, 52.

Carnes, Patrick J. *Contrary to Love.* Minneapolis, Minn.: CompCare Publishers, 1989.

————. *Don't Call It Love.* New York: Bantam Books, 1991.

Earlc, Ralph, and Crow, Gregory. *Lonely All the Time: Recognizing, Understand and Overcoming Sex Addiction, for Addicts and Codependents.* New York: The Phillip Lief Group, Inc., 1989.

L'Abate, L., et al. *Handbook of Differential Treatments for Addictions.* Boston: Allyn and Bacon, 1992.

Milkman, H., and S. Sunderwirth. *Craving for Ecstasy: The Chemistry and Consciousness of Escape.* Lexington, Mass.: Lexington Books, 1987.

Schwartz, M. "Sexual Compulsivity as Post-Traumatic Stress Disorder: Treatment Perspectives." *Psychiatric Annals* 22 (1992): 6.

Sunderwirth, G., and H. Milkman. "Behavior and Neurochemical Commonalities in Addiction." *Contemporary Family Therapy* (Oct. 1991).

Wilson, Peter, ed. *Principals and Practice of Relapse Prevention.* New York: The Guilford Press, 1992.

Trauma Blocking

Blizard, Ruth A., and Ann M. Bluhm "Attachment to the Abuser: Integrating Object-Relations and Trauma Theories in Treatment of Abuse Survivors." *Psychotherapy* 31, no. 3 (1994): 383.

Buchanan, L., and W. Buchanan. "Eating Disorders: Bulimia and Anorexia." *Handbook of Differential Treatments for Addictions.* Boston: Allyn and Bacon, 1992.

Edwall, G., N. Hoffman, and P. Harrison. "Psychological Correlates of Sexual Abuse in Adolescent Girls in Chemical Dependency Treatment." *Adolescence* (Summer 1989).

Evans, K., and J. M. Sullivan. *Dual Diagnosis: Counseling the Mentally Ill Substance Abuser.* New York: The Guilford Press (1990).

Evans, S., and S. Shaefer. "Incest and Chemically Dependent Women: Treatment Implications." *Journal of Chemical Dependency Treatment* 1, no. 1 (1987).

Feinauer, Leslie L. "Comparison of Long-Term Effects of Child Abuse by Type of Abuse and by Relationship of the Offender and the Victim." *The American Journal of Family Therapy* 17, no. 1 (1989): 48–56.

Hagen, T. "A Retrospective Search for the Etiology of Drug Abuse: A Background Comparison of a Drug-Addicted Population of Women and a Control Group of Non-Addicted Women." *National Institute on Drug Abuse: Research Monograph Series* (1988): Mono 81.

Miller, B. A., W. R. Downs, and D. M. Gondoli. "Delinquency, Childhood Violence, and the Development of Alcoholism in Women." *Crime and Delinquency* 35, no. 1 (1989).

Rohsenow, D. J., R. Corbett, and D. Devine. "Molested as Children: A Hidden Contribution to Substance Abuse?" *Journal of Substance Abuse Treatment* 5, no. 1 (1988).

Root, M. "Treatment Failures: The Role of Sexual Victimization in Women's Addictive Behavior." *American Journal of Ortopsychiatrics* (Oct. 1989).

Shaefer, M. R., K. Sobieraj, and R. L. Hollyfield. "Prevalence of Childhood Physical Abuse in Adult Male Veteran Alcoholics." *Child Abuse and Neglect* 12 (1988).

Sullivan, E. J. "Associations Between Chemical Dependency and Sexual Problems in Nurses." *Journal of Interpersonal Violence* 3, no. 3 (1988).

Trauma Splitting

Bliss, Eugene. *Multiple Personality, Allied Disorders and Hypnosis.* New York: Oxford University Press, 1986.

Braun, B. G., M.D., ed. *The Treatment of Multiple Personality Disorder.* Washington, D.C.: American Psychiatric Press, 1986.

Briere, John. *Child Abuse Trauma: Theory and Treatment of the Lasting Effects.* Newbury Park, Mass.: SAGE Publications, 1992.

Foy, D. ed. *Treating PTSD: Cognitive-Behavioral Strategies.* New York: The Guilford Press, 1992.

Herman, Judith Lewis. *Trauma and Recovery.* New York: Basic Books, 1992.

Kluft, Richard, M.D. *Childhood Antecedents of Multiple Personality Disorder.* Washington, D.C.: American Psychiatric Press, 1985.

————. "First Rank—Symptoms as a Diagnostic Clue to Multiple Personality Disorder." *American Journal of Psychiatry* 144 (1985): 293–298.

————. *The Natural History of Multiple Personality Disorder in Childhood Antecedent of Multiple Personality.* Washington, D.C.: American Psychiatric Press, 1985.

Lew, Michael. *Victims No Longer: Men Recovering from Incest and Other Sexual Child Abuse.* New York: Harper and Row, 1988.

Putnam, Frank W. *Diagnosis and Treatment of Multiple Personality Disorder.* New York: Guilford Press, 1989.

————. *Recent Research on Multiple Personality Disorder.* Psychiatric Clinics North America, 1991.

Ross, Colin A. *Multiple Personality Disorder, Diagnosis, Clinical Features and Treatment.* New York: John Wiley and Sons, 1989.

van der Kolk, Bessel. *Psychological Trauma.* Washington, D.C.: American Psychiatric Press, 1987.

Young, W. "Observations on Fantasy in the Formation of Multiple Personality Disorder." *Dissociation* 1 (1988): 13–20.

————. "Psychodynamics and Dissociation: All That Switches Is Not Split." *Dissociation* 1 (1988): 33–38.

Trauma Abstinence

Abramson, E., and G. Lucido. "Childhood Sexual Experience and Bulimia." *Addictive Behaviors* 16 (1991).

Buchanan, L., and W. Buchanan. "Eating Disorders: Bulimia and Anorexia." *Handbook of Differential Treatments for Addictions.* Boston: Allyn and Bacon, 1992.

Covington, Stephanie. *Awakening Your Sexuality: A Guide for Recovering Women.* San Francisco: HarperCollins, 1991.

Fossum, M., and M. Mason. *Facing Shame: Families in Recovery.* New York: W.W. Norton & Company, 1986.

Gil, Eliana. *The Healing Power of Play.* New York: The Guilford Press, 1991.

Goldfarb, L. "Sexual Abuse Antecedent to Anorexia Nervosa, Bulimia, and Compulsive Overeating: Three Case Reports." *International Journal of Eating* 6, no. 5 (1987): 675–680.

Irons, Richard, M.D., and Mark Laaser, Ph.D. "The Abduction of Fidelity: Sexual Exploitation by Clergy—Experience with Inpatient Assessment." *Sexual Addiction and Compulsivity: The Journal of Treatment and Prevention* 1, no. 2 (1994): 119–129.

Maltz, W. *The Sexual Healing Journey: A Guide for Survivors of Sexual Abuse.* New York: HarperCollins, 1991.

Maltz, W., and B. Holman. *Incest and Sexuality: A Guide to Understanding and Healing.* Lexington, Mass.: Lexington Books, 1987.

Trauma Shame

Bradshaw, John. *Healing the Shame That Binds You.* Deerfield Beach, Fla.: Health Communications, Inc., 1988.

Carlsen, Mary Baird. *Meaning-Making: The Therapeutic Processes in Adult Development.* New York: W.W. Norton & Company, 1988.

Fossum, M., and M. Mason. *Facing Shame: Families in Recovery.* New York: W.W. Norton & Company, 1986.

Harper, James, and Margaret Hoopes. *Uncovering Shame: An Approach Integrating Individuals and Their Family Systems.* New York: W.W. Norton & Company, 1990.

Kaufman, G. *The Psychology of Shame: Theory and Treatment of Shame-Based Syndromes.* New York: Springer Publishing Company, 1989.

Trauma Repetition

Foy, D., ed. *Treating PTSD: Cognitive-Behavior Strategies.* New York: The Guilford Press, 1992.

Love, P. *The Emotional Incest Syndrome: What to Do When a Parent's Love Rules Your Life.* New York: Bantam Books, 1990.

Money, John. *Lovemaps: Clinical Concepts of Sexual/Erotic Health and Pathology, Paraphilia, and Gender Transposition in Childhood, Adolescence, and Maturity.* New York: Irvington Publishers, Inc., 1988.

Schwartz, M. "Sexual Compulsivity as Post-Traumatic Stress Disorder: Treatment Perspectives." *Psychiatric Annals* 22, no. 6 (1992).

Trauma Bonds

De Young, Mary, and Judith Lowry. "Traumatic Bonding: Clinical Implications in Incest." *Child Welfare League of America* LXXI (1992): 165–175.

Feinauer, L. "Comparison of Long-Term Effects of Child Abuse by Type of Abuse and by Relationship of the Offender to the Victim." *The American Journal of Family Therapy* 17, no. 1 (1989): 48–56.

Graham, Dee L. R., with Edna I. Rawlings, and Roberta K. Rigsby. *Loving to Survive*. New York: New York University Press, 1994.

Gutheil, T. "Patients Involved in Sexual Misconduct with Therapists: Is a Victim Profile Possible?" *Psychiatric Annals* 21, no. 11 (1991): 661–665.

Herman, Judith Lewis. *Trauma and Recovery*. New York: Basic Books, 1992.

Lemieu, Andrine M., M.A., and Christopher L. Coe, Ph.D. "Abuse-Related Post-Traumatic Stress Disorder: Evidence for Chronic Neuroendocrine Activation in Women." *Psychosomatic Medicine* 57, (1995): 105.

Russell, D. "The Prevalence and Seriousness of Incestuous Abuse: Stepfathers vs. Biological Fathers." *Child Abuse and Neglect* 8 (1985): 15–22.

Seat, J., J. Trent, and K. Jwa. *Journal of Pastoral Care* 47 (Winter 1993): 363–370.

Terr, L. "Chowchilla Revisited: The Effects of Psychic Trauma Four Years After a School-Bus Kidnapping." *The American Journal of Psychiatry* 140. 12 (1983).

van der Kolk, Bessel. "The Trauma Spectrum: The Interaction of Biological and Social Events in the Genesis of the Trauma Response." *Journal of Traumatic Stress* 1, no.3 (1988).

Vogt, Amanda. "Cults Get Mainstream Makeover." *The Arizona Republic*, 26 April, 1997: sec. R, p. 2.

West, Malcom, Ph.D., and Adrienne E. R. Sheldon, B.A. "Classification of Pathological Attachment Patterns in Adults." *Journal of Personality Disorders* 2, no. 2 (1988): 153–159.

Index

Index

243

recovery
arousal recovery plan, 179–180
blocking recovery plan, 180–182
defining self, 209–210
deprivation recovery plan, 187–190
dimensions of, 165–166
grieving, 204
guided imagery, 213–216
honesty, 206–207
implementing boundaries, 202
misperception of others, 200–201
path of full relationship, 159–165
path of limited contact, 154–159
path of no contact, 148–154
plan, 153
plan for compulsive relationships, 167–170
reactivity recovery plan, 174–178
relapse prevention plan, 172
remaining in reality, 199–200
repetition recovery plan, 192–196
risks, 198–199
self-responsibility, 210–211
shame recovery plan, 191–192
solitude, 204–205
spirituality, 205–206
splitting recovery plan, 182–187
suffering to meaning, 211–212
vulnerability, 207–208
willingness to fight, 208–209
rejection, compulsive, 126
repetition compulsion, 24, 33, 192
risk, 3
role-playing, 158
Ryan, Congressman Leo, 89–90, 103

S
sado-masochism, 10, 155. See also sex addiction
satiation, 13
Scheele, Rochelle, 152
secrets, 10, 30, 99
seduction, 29, 65
"scripts," 55–56

susceptibility of dysfunctional persons, 54
terror, relationship between, 57–58
"Your History of Seduction" exercise, 70–72
self-destructive behavior, 22
self-hatred, 21, 22
self-mutilation, 22
self-reliance, compulsive, 126
serenity prayer, 142
sex addiction, 9–10, 15, 84
anonymous sex, 10
high-risk sex, 10, 11, 14
inappropriate caregiver/care receiver relationships, 10, 57, 82–83, 85
prostitution. see prostitution
sado-masochism, 10
sex offending, 10
sexual abuse, 7, 14, 20, 25, 26, 93, 100, 114, 160. See also incest
addictive high-risk sex as adults, 9–10
children's coping mechanisms, 14–15
by clergy. see clergy misconduct
reluctance to report, 61
sexual addiction, 29, 79, 80, 118, 162
bingeing, 30
case study, 161–165
compulsive sexual violence, 80
denial, relationship between, 114
high-risk sex, 24
sexual assault
reluctance to report, 59
sexual avoidance, 12, 20, 30, 32
sexual harassment, 60, 91–92
Anita Hill/Clarence Thomas case, 61, 111
case study, 1–3
reluctance to report, 60–61
sexual offenders
clergy. see clergy misconduct
number of offenses, 67

About the Author

Patrick J. Carnes, Ph.D., C.A.S., is a nationally known speaker on addiction and recovery issues. He is author of *Out of the Shadows: Understanding Sexual Addiction, Revised Edition* (1992); *Contrary to Love: Helping the Sexual Addict* (1989); *A Gentle Path Through the Twelve Steps: For All People in the Process of Recovery, Revised Edition* (1993); and *Don't Call It Love: Recovery from Sexual Addiction* (1991). Experts regard his first book on family systems, entitled *Understanding Us,* as a classic in family education. It is now available in many foreign editions.

Dr. Carnes is clinical director for sexual disorder services at The Meadows in Wickenburg, Arizona. The Meadows built its educational and therapeutic services for sexual disorders on the technology that evolved from Dr. Carnes's landmark study of the recoveries of 1,000 sex addicts. The *New Age Journal* described *Don't Call It Love* and the work summarized in it as "the best book on the market about addiction and its costs and consequences." His latest book, *Sexual Anorexia: Overcoming Sexual Self-Hatred,* has been described by *The New Times* as creating "a new wave of understanding about sexuality."

Dr. Carnes is the editor-in-chief of *Sexual Addiction and Compulsivity: The Journal of Treatment and Prevention,* a

Brunner/Mazel publication and the official journal of the
National Council of Sexual Addiction/Compulsivity. Dr.
Carnes also serves as a board member of the organization.

Dr. Carnes serves on the national advisory board of the
American Academy of Health Care Providers in the Addictive
Disorders. The Academy is a national certification organization for clinical professionals, founded to determine
standards of training and clinical experience in the field of
addiction treatment.

Previously, Dr. Carnes designed the sexual dependency unit
at Golden Valley Health Center in Golden Valley, Minnesota.
This unit was the first inpatient facility in the country for the
treatment of sexual addiction.

Dr. Carnes is the founding chairman of the board of
directors for Cardinal Health Systems in Edina, Minnesota.
Cardinal develops innovative diagnostic and educational
systems for family practice and internal medicine physicians.

Dr. Carnes was also director of development for human
services at Fairview-Southdale Hospital in Minneapolis. His
responsibilities included broadening family programming
concepts in mental health and pastoral care. He also was
director of the hospital's Family Renewal Center, a program
for families affected by chemical dependency, eating disorders
and sexual addiction. In his role, he was a key co-investigator
of a five-year study of family sexual abuse funded by the
National Center of Child Abuse and Neglect.

Dr. Carnes's experience includes three years of teaching in
a counselor training program at Metropolitan Community
College, Minneapolis; working for Personnel Decisions, Inc.,
a nationally known group of industrial psychologists; and
serving as director of a crisis intervention and counseling
agency for adolescents. Dr. Carnes has consulted with a wide
range of groups within business, academic, military, social
service and criminal justice settings.

Dr. Carnes graduated in 1966 from St. John's University, Collegeville, Minnesota, with a bachelor of arts. He received his master's degree in 1969 from Brown University, and a doctorate in counselor education and organizational development from the University of Minnesota in 1980.

Bestsellers from HCI

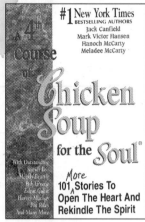
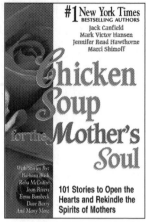

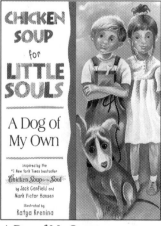